NINE ROOMS

Laura

Thank you so much for your care and attention with this text. It really shines through!

Dr John Rowe

14/06/2021

First published in 2021 by John Rowe Coaching

ISBN 978-1-9168881-0-4

Cover and book design by Tom Howey

www.johnrowecoaching.com
www.ninerooms.co.uk

Nine Rooms

Mastering the Missing Dimension to Coaching, Teaching and Counselling

Dr John Rowe

Introduction

There is a missing dimension to how we understand face-to-face communication that could transform the helping professions. It is rarely taught, but it can be. Once mastered, it can inspire growth in ways you may not have yet imagined. It can support your skills and take your successes to another level. This dimension is not a theoretical, philosophical or ethereal concept floating somewhere in the air: it's a tangible reality, hidden in plain sight, that profoundly affects what we do every day.

You may not be aware of this dimension because of the limitations your profession puts upon itself when it comes to valuing 'different' ideas. Your profession exists within a type of bubble where unconventional practices must be explained in conventional ways if they are to be taken seriously. And here lies the rub. What if these systems can't actually be interpreted in this way? Wouldn't ideas with massive potential for growth inevitably be silenced? It is up to us to recognise the harm this does. Only we can change the parameters of our craft.

In science, people are making extraordinary leaps forward by stepping outside of their bubbles into the unknown. The real question is: do you have a yearning to do the same? In terms of communication techniques, do you have the feeling that your profession may have exhausted its original ideas when it comes to leaps in authentic growth? Is your profession chipping away at old blocks and regurgitating the 'same old, same old' in different guises to create the illusion of progress? Does your bubble conveniently ignore the fact that your students' and clients' progress has levelled out or is even on the decline? What if it's time to step outside, take a deep breath and have a proper look around at some new possibilities?

Nine Rooms offers you the opportunity to do just that. It's a chance to stick your head above the parapet and experience an invigorating gust of cold air. It may provoke you and challenge your usual patterns of thought, but it will open your mind to the potential of communication and re-energise you. You will learn in an entirely new way, but we will start slowly, from the beginning: the ABCs of the missing dimension to communication. Although it might seem daunting at first, you will in fact be able to incorporate your understanding into your practice instantly. It will not replace your existing learning or interfere with the requirements of your job; it will exist happily alongside them and raise your game to another level. As you will see, working with an understanding of the missing dimension creates improved wellbeing and a nourished environment. It does so without causing conflict or confrontation.

I discovered this practice in 1995, on a trip to China. I'd heard of different approaches to coaching, to teaching and learning, and wanted to experience them first-hand. In the Wudang mountains, I did. Alongside a Taoist master, in a damp room shared with rats, I began to experience another dynamic to coaching. The teacher could lift everyone present in the room, in complete and real terms, from under the surface, consistently. And, as the weeks passed, his influence only grew. Its impact transcended professional practice. Once home, I wanted to communicate this skill, but I didn't know how.

Twenty-five years later, after a shift from teaching to coaching, with a doctorate, a master coach qualification and a counselling diploma under my belt, I'm here, ready to give an explanation of the missing dimension a go. Although it's very difficult to explain, the good news is that it's worth the effort. I've found it to be extremely effective in the reality of today's coaching, teaching, counselling and helping environments. In fact, it will be an invaluable tool in any situation where anyone wants to inspire anyone else towards improved results. If you are unafraid of stepping out and trying something new, then *Nine Rooms* may be what you have been searching for.

While our professions are not approaching an eleventh-hour scenario, we are certainly heading towards the tenth. As our organisations cave to the paranoia of accountability, where form-filling, report writing, league tables and databases are more important than the creation of authentic relationships, we arrive at a crossroads. We can either shine a light on to other traditions that can solve our issues by addressing them in fundamentally different ways, or we can stay safely within our professional bubbles looking nervously over our shoulders and hoping to somehow find our answers there.

The choice is ours. The choice is yours.

Notes on the Presentation

As you might have guessed, a book exploring a different dimension to communication needs to be constructed in a certain way. Based on the Taoist tradition, I have written stories for you that sit amongst diagrams, examples and explanations. These, in juxtaposition, contain your learning. It may be a different way of absorbing targeted information, but as Oran Harari said, 'The electric light did not come from the continuous improvement of candles.' Sometimes we need to take an entirely different approach to our understanding in order to shake up our ways of thinking.

This style of learning is all about your emotional responses rather than working things out intellectually. That 'working things out' bit has already been done for you. All that is required is for you to make your way slowly but surely on a journey through the rooms, giving yourself plenty of time for things to rise and settle. The examples I have given are mainly from coaching, teaching and counselling, because these are my crafts. Replace these with your own environments and specialisms if you are outside of these fields. You will be able to think of many examples, I'm sure. They are everywhere.

Finally, attempt to let go of your profession's established way of thinking, at least for the duration of the book. Try not to compare the 'different' you may find in the rooms to your established 'known'. Leave yourself open to enjoying a gently undulating train ride to somewhere new, whose experience is all encompassing.

See you on the other side.

Nine Rooms

This is the way.

The Outer Chambers

The first room is not quite ready yet.

Please enjoy the story of *Ting & His Cats*
while you are waiting.

Ting & His Cats

There was a monk called Ting. He looked after the stray cats that wandered into the monastery. Ting was not the brightest spark in the box. He could not cook or clean, and although he was successful with the begging bowl, he almost always gave the food away before he got back to the monastery to share it. Ting was well looked after by the other monks, as people like Ting often tend to be, especially by those in the know.

Ting got to know the nature of his cats very well. Every day the monks would ask Ting if his cats were being respectfully behaved, and every day he would politely answer 'yes', although once a ginger tom drank from the sacred spring and he had to tell him off, so that day he had to politely answer 'no'. Ting enjoyed the antics of his cats, their ins and outs, daily. Whether they bathed in the sun or paraded around the courtyard, they always made him happy. Sometimes outsiders would visit and ask him for his advice on their cats, which was always given freely and respectfully.

The door is now open for you.

The rule of the rooms:

it is unwise to run ahead.

Room One

A small room in an ancient temple complex.

The shutters are closed, but light streams in through the gaps.

A large flat-screen television is mounted on the wall. It flickers on.

Look to the screen
and follow the instructions.

Take a line.

Mark the centre of your line.

Know that your line represents the art of communication.

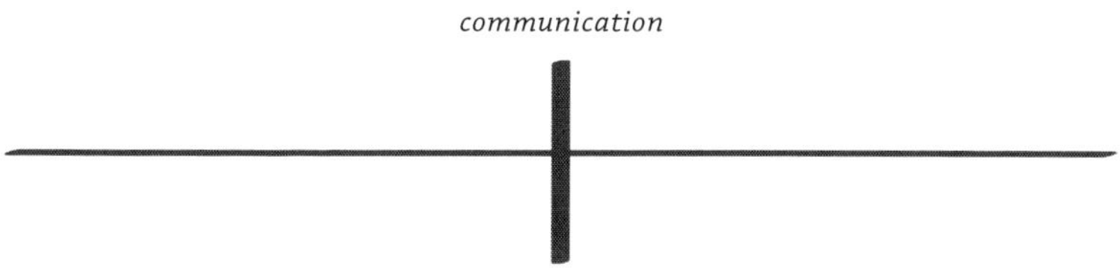

The left-hand side of your line is communication being understood by breaking the subject down into smaller and smaller pieces – into more and more detail. It is how we traditionally like to define communication.

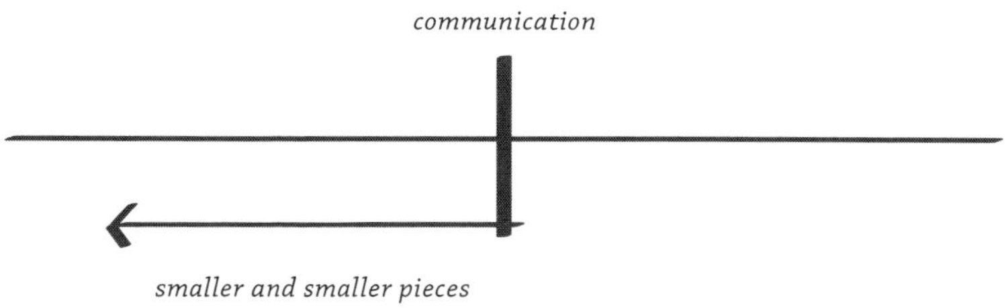

Here you are encouraged to assume that the more detail in which you are able to describe something, the better that thing is understood by you. Such an approach is likely to be the way you have been taught to recognise learning of value at school. It is a compartmentalised approach where describable details, methodologies, philosophies and theories fit into a series of definable and explainable boxes that represent your knowledge on the subject.

The right-hand side of the line is communication being understood by *not* breaking it down. 'Communication' remains entirely intact and whole, in its natural, unaffected motion. (Think of a tree growing as a single unit, rather than as the sum of its parts.)

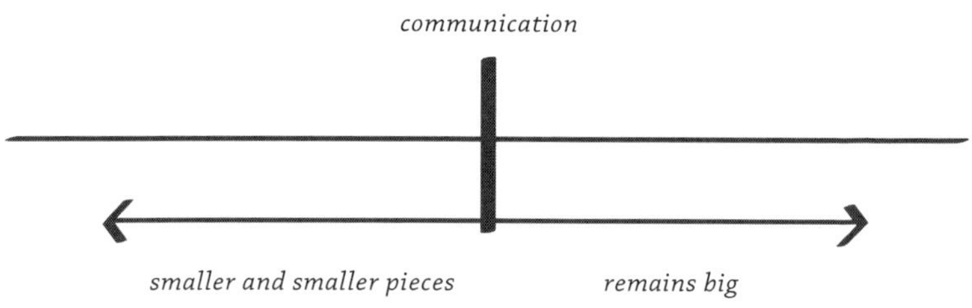

While the left-hand side of the equation values the describable qualities of communication, the right-hand side values the indescribable immediacy of the communication experience. From the right-hand perspective communication cannot be described because it is too busy being experienced moment to moment.

Take the communication of feelings. From the left-hand side of the line, feelings are describable. They can be defined: ‘happy’ and ‘sad’, ‘joyous’ and ‘melancholy’. They can be analysed, reflected upon and recorded. From the right-hand side of the line, feelings are not able to be described because, when it comes to the fullness of a feeling as it is being experienced, words cannot come close. In fact, none of the experience of reality, as it is being lived, can be accurately described, if at all. It is a vast area where the immediacy of our moment to moment existence is present only in its naturally indescribable state.

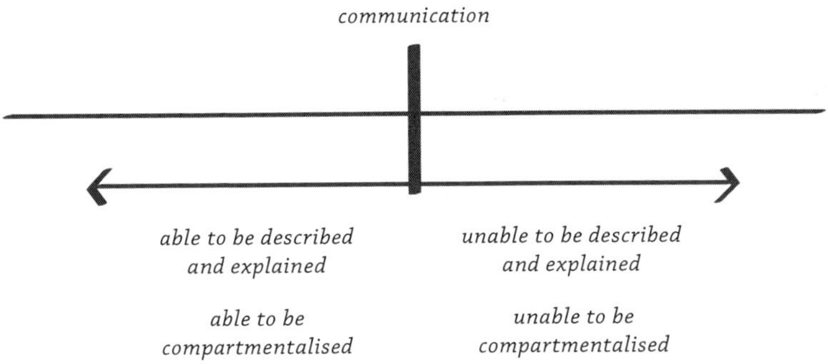

To summarise, the left-hand side of the line is a place where communication is described. Here it can be analysed and studied objectively, from a distance. The right-hand side of the line is a place where communication is experienced. It exists only in the continuous, moment to moment stream of communication being lived.

Presented for your consideration (and amusement) is the story of Ms Ming.

Ms Ming & Her Magnificent Knowledge

There was once a dedicated teacher called Ms Ming. She was called 'Ms Ming with magnificent knowledge'. It was not a name given to her by her students (they called her something else entirely). It was a name she had given herself. Ms Ming always shared her magnificent knowledge wherever she went – with the teachers in the staff room, with the parents at the school gate, even with those waiting in queues at the store or at the market. How generous she was. Those that knew of her moved away quickly when she entered a room, and those that she caught unawares would find a reason to leave abruptly for an urgent engagement.

Ms Ming died never once knowing that more important than imparting knowledge was the ability to inspire others to want to listen.

Poor Ms Ming.

The story of Ms Ming reveals that a teacher who focuses only on the left-hand side of the line (and not the right) encounters problems. In the case of Ms Ming, she valued the describable and explainable (in the form of her subject knowledge) at the expense of the indescribable and unexplainable (her ability to connect, moment to moment, with her students). Sadly, by ignoring the latter, she lost touch with the reality of what she wanted to achieve: to be an excellent communicator of knowledge. Ignoring the importance of the indescribable side of the craft of teaching has come at a price: blindness to the bigger picture.

As the story says, 'Poor Ms Ming'.

When it comes to communication (essentially a lived experience – unique, personal and in the moment), if we value only the explainable side of the equation, we do not come close to addressing communication in action.

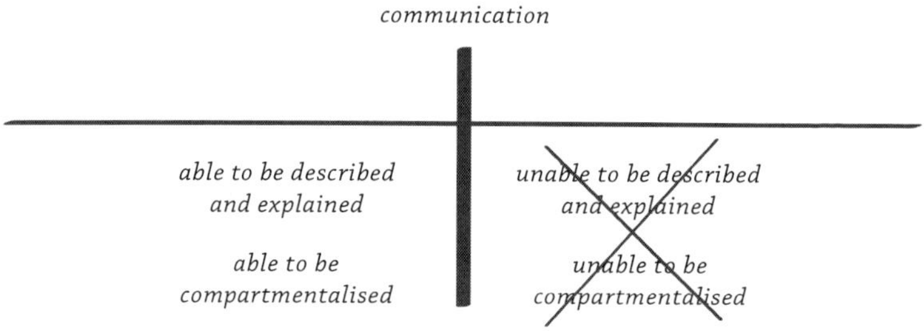

Sometimes the relevance of the unexplainable can feel so distant that it more or less disappears off the radar. The picture becomes one-sided, unbalanced and distorted. An environment is then created where the describable alone dictates our values: what is good and bad, right and wrong.

Examples of relying on the describable at the expense of the indescribable may take many forms. As a parent, we might read too many books on how to raise a child and, in doing so, devalue the importance of the natural drive and intuition of parenthood; in counselling we might become overly attached to a certain methodology to the point where we begin to believe that our client's progress only exists in established, compartmentalised and explainable forms; in coaching we might be over-invested in certain linear models in the mistaken belief that progress can only occur in a linear way; in management and leadership we might invest in our technique to the point that we a hide behind a façade rather than being our authentic selves; in nursing we might get used to focusing on the technical side of our patients' recoveries while forgetting the importance of personal connection to the healing process.

The technical and describable are, of course, of immense value. Nobody would want to visit a surgeon or a therapist who does not know their stuff.

Please enjoy the story of Mrs J. Chen PhD, to explore this idea further.

Dr J. Chen & Her Indescribable Quality

Mrs J. Chen, PhD, was a wonderful counsellor. She would study the techniques of her profession for hours every week and would always keep up to date. She was the chair of two very important committees and would appear at seminars regularly. Her papers in journals were exemplary, and her books were noteworthy examples of her counselling expertise in practice. Mrs Chen was so successful that she would often have to make her clients' appointments early in the mornings and late into the evenings. Her clients would sometimes say that they felt as if they were floating on air after being counselled by her.

Despite attending all her lectures and reading all of her articles and books, nobody ever came close to repeating Mrs Chen's success. They did not think it important to note that Mrs Chen had written something a little different in her first book which might shed light on what was setting her apart: 'There is definitely something happening in my sessions that I cannot describe. I fear, if I do describe it, that it will stop, and I will be left powerless.'

The story of Mrs Chen represents the two sides of the equation, the describable and the indescribable, working together.

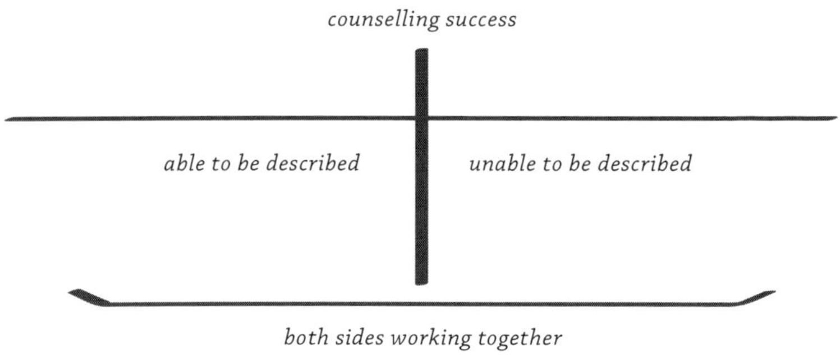

Mrs Chen greatly values the describable elements of her counselling. They are an ongoing passion. She is renowned for her knowledge. The counsellor also values the indescribable nature of her counselling to the point where she says that to describe it would be to negatively impact her practice. She leaves that area alone. Mrs Chen knows that it is the combination of the indescribable alongside her exceptional technical knowledge that results in her enormous success.

To summarise, just because something cannot be described does not mean it is not of immense value to your profession.

Questions begin to appear on the screen.

- *How do you imagine it is that Mrs Chen's students cannot emulate her exceptional success in working with clients?*

- *In teaching, coaching and counselling, and in all of the helping professions, the technical and describable elements of our crafts are essential, but where do you currently stand when it comes to the importance of the indescribable? Are you more a Ms Ming or a Mrs Chen?*

To help with your ponderances, presented here is the story of Jon.

Jon & His Acting

When Jon was a young boy, he was a charismatic performer. He would invent plays in his garden and the neighbours would clap and cheer from the other side of the fences. When he went to school, he was always given the leading roles in the annual shows. The audience looked forward to seeing him and praised him very highly for his magnetism and passion. It was fair to say that Jon was incredibly watchable. When he went to secondary school Jon took on harder plays. Many in the audience commented that he was the most engaging youngster they had ever seen perform.

Being inexperienced, technique was not Jon's strong point. Sometimes he would face the back instead of the front if the other actor was standing behind him. Sometimes he would be too loud, and at other times he would be too soft. Sometimes he would even stand outside of the spotlight and could not be seen at all. Nevertheless, captivated, the audience still clapped and cheered when he bowed.

On the advice of his teacher, Jon went to study drama at a special acting school. He had to audition, but he got in straightaway due to his charismatic nature. In the first year Jon studied vocal technique and movement. In the second year Jon studied monologues and characterisation. In the third year Jon got to use his learning to once again perform in plays.

This time Jon did not lift the audience. They admired his technique greatly but went home impressed rather than inspired. In separating technique from his natural charisma (the thing that filled the stage and made Jon special), Jon's magnetism was gone.

All the school had to do was to teach Jon technique while respecting the value of his natural charisma, always being aware of both so they could grow seamlessly together. Instead, the school prioritised what was missing, the technique, and, in doing so, systematically destroyed the thing that made Jon special. The indescribable thing that gave Jon life, that might have been his life, was gone.

Jon lived for a long time, well into his nineties, but he died unfulfilled. His grave was not that of a great actor but of a factory worker. Unseen by human eyes, the spirits wrote on his stone 'Never restrict the indescribable whole by improving the describable parts.'

There is a hardwood chair in the room, faded blue.

You sit and take a breath.

You take time to ponder again:

- *Dare you take an honest look at how you are impacting the indescribable qualities of your children, patients, athletes, students and clients?*
- *How much would you like to resolve this issue?*
- *What if a resolution could be found that causes no conflict or confrontation whatsoever?*
- *Will you believe that the Nine Rooms can show you how?*

When you are pondering the answers to your questions (and the many others throughout the rooms) always remember to:

- ponder with a sense of lightness and humour.
- not to judge or blame yourself or others – just notice.
- let the ideas come and then let them go. Do not hold on to anything for later or write anything down.

The light in the room is fading.

You can choose to stay in the room, if you like. If you do, the screen will reappear and the lesson will be retold, but your experience will be different – more certain.

If you are ready to continue onwards, this is the way.

You may, of course, decide to leave the rooms at this juncture. The missing dimension might not be your cup of tea. No hard feelings. Hope to see you again sometime.

As you are travelling to the second room, please be entertained by the stage magician, Wu.

The Magnificent, Magical Wu

Wu thinks he is dressed like a real wizard, although he is not. Well, not like any wizard you might know. Wu has a tall hat embroidered with glittered stars and moons, a gown of heavy grey silk and a black wand with a white tip. Wu is a stage wizard and is every inch the genuine article. If he was a real wizard, he would certainly give wizards a bad name. Wu makes grand gestures and throws glitter and powder all over the place. His incantations use the most appalling rhymes.

Wu waves his right arm, and out of thin air appears a green egg. Then he waves his arm again, and another egg appears that is purple, then one that is pink. Out of thin air. 'What? Is Wu a wizard after all? The Magnificent, Magical Wu: a wizard!' The audience clap and cheer. 'Wu is doing the impossible.' 'Wu is making things appear from nowhere.' 'Wu is incredible.' 'He is indeed the Magnificent, Magical Wu!'

Wu takes a long, deep, flamboyant bow. Then he takes another longer, deeper and even more flamboyant bow with arms circling everywhere. It lasts so long that it could be a play. Eventually he stands upright and smiles. Something is about to happen – but what? Slowly Wu draws his sleeves up to his elbows. Revealed are two leather braces strapped to his wrists, each holding coloured eggs. The audience, never having seen this type of reveal of a trick before, become confused. Wu continues his demonstration. In slow motion, he lifts his right arm above his head, and the audience's eyes follow. Wu coughs, then coughs again, nodding towards his left arm. He is drawing the audience's attention away from where they are currently looking. They mutter amongst themselves and switch their gaze to the left. Then, from his left hand, Wu skilfully launches an egg with his fingers, upwards into the air, and catches it in his right palm. The audience begin to realise that if they just look one way, at Wu's right hand, the egg seems to appear out of thin air, even though it was thrown from the left. Well done Wu! The audience sees that there is indeed no magic: no appearing egg. It is just that they have been looking in entirely the wrong direction. Clever, clever Wu.

Wu is only a stage magician after all. He cannot make the impossible appear. But Wu does know one thing: what seems impossible can become possible if you open yourself up to the whole picture rather than just focusing on where we 'know' the answer should be.

As if by magic, the door to your next room appears.

Room Two

The room is vast. There is an expanse of wall in front of you. Projected on it are the words:

It's all a matter of perspective.

Underneath appears:

So, where do you stand?

There is a low bench by the window.

You sit on the bench for a while.

You ponder.

So far, there are at least three clues to the missing dimension:

- It sits within the immediacy of your communicative relationships.
- It is indescribable.
- It cannot be taught or learnt by traditional techniques.

Something else occurs to you:

- The missing dimension sits within your lived experience, so it is intrinsically personal.

Then a sentence appears on the wall as if in response to your thoughts. It says something you may have expected.

"You need to know more about the nature of the right-hand side of the line."

Followed by:

"But first you need to study the left-hand side of the line, for comparison and context."

A helpful instruction appears:

"Place yourself on the left-hand side of the equation."

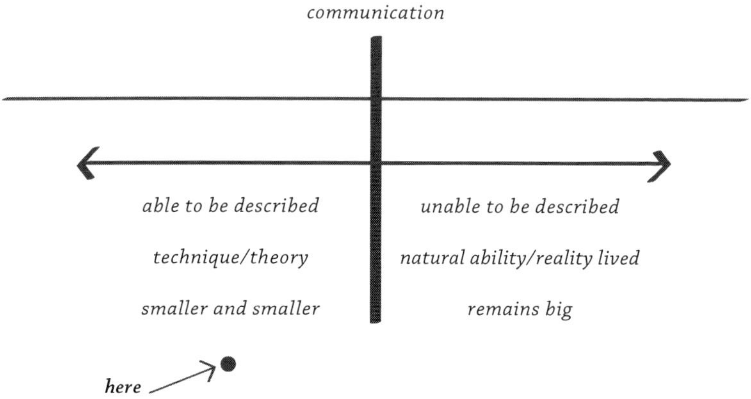

Your position dictates your field of view, for now. It is unlikely to be where you place yourself in your practice, but try to imagine only understanding the communicative nature of your craft from a detailed and technical standpoint.

You consider the story about the monkey.

The Men & the Monkey

There were once two men, in the olden days, who were intrigued by the nature of the monkey. They would often sit under trees for hours watching the monkeys play and enjoying their screams and shouts. They were so impressed by their energetic shenanigans that one evening the friends decided to find out what made the monkeys tick. They shot a single monkey down from the tree with an anaesthetic dart and waited until the animal was asleep. Once unconscious they swiftly cut off the monkey's head to examine inside. After an hour or so of full body dissection, intrigued by what they found, they carefully stitched the monkey back together and waited for her to recover. But they could not wake the monkey up.

These men were not cruel, they were ignorant. They did not understand the importance of life to their studies and so mistakenly killed their subject.

You: 'What?'

Thoughts appear as questions:

- *Can everything we do be understood by dissecting it?*
- *Can anything we do be understood by dissecting it?*
- *From your current left-hand technical and theoretical perspective, can communication be taken apart, worked upon, and successfully put back together again without being significantly altered?*

You need an example and so one appears on the wall.

"Consider confident communication.
What does it mean to you?"

Confident communication in its essentially personal and indescribably raw state, sits only on one side of the line – the right. Because it is being lived, moment to moment, it can only exist here. But, from a coaching perspective, for confident communication to be worked upon, it first needs to be identified as such, and so it becomes labelled – put in a box, ready to be discussed between coach and client. In that instant, confident communication is moved from one side of the equation to the other. From its naturally indefinable state, it is transferred to a place where it can be described, and in doing so, it is transformed. What is now being worked upon by you and your client, athlete, student or child, is not the raw experience of confident communication in its natural state, because in this state it is indescribable. Instead, you have developed a version of confident communication that is compartmentalised.

Consider this story.

The Ranger & the Cheetah

There was once a park ranger in Africa whose job was to oversee the safety of the cheetahs on the plains. For twenty years he watched them and guarded them. They were wild animals in their natural habitat and it took a long time for him to be accepted by them, upwind and from a safe distance. After he retired, the ranger came to hear that some of his cheetahs had been taken out of the wild 'for their own sakes' and placed in captivity. So, he took it upon himself to visit them, to once again be close to his animals. On arrival he saw two of his cheetahs in a cage – and his heart broke. They barely moved other than to walk in tight patterns. They were not the creatures he knew at all.

The sign on the cage said 'research animals'. The ranger wondered what sort of research was being carried out. You couldn't understand a cheetah in the wild by examining a cheetah in a cage. You couldn't. Not at all. You would get completely the wrong idea. The ranger went to find a keeper to ask him about the project. On hearing the query, the young keeper smiled condescendingly, and in a voice edged with pity he explained to the older man that the research was too complicated for a simple ranger to understand and so it was best he didn't try. The ranger nodded, lifted his hat, and walked away.

At ninety-three the ranger went to sleep, in an old chair, and drifted upwards. On his way he saw his beloved plains, and at a safe distance, upwind, there were wild cheetahs. 'So, this is heaven,' he thought. 'This is heaven.'

You lean against the wall and ponder:

- ❖ *How different is reading about love to the experience of being in love?*
- ❖ *If confident communication only fully exists in the immediacy of our lived experience, so must the opposite: the confidence problems of our children,*

clients, teams and students. If we look to correct a confidence issue only from the left-hand side of the line, where confidence cannot even come close to being fully described, how can we possibly help our clients in real terms with their moment to moment problem?

- *Can you catch a feeling in your hand, put it in a box, and save it for later?*

- *Consider how you talk about confidence with your clients, students, athletes or children. Are you addressing confidence as an intrinsic, indescribable part of who they are, in a state in which it is 'alive', or are you studying confidence as a labelled and artificially held concept, to the extent that it could be described as something entirely different: 'dead'?*

From our left-hand perspective, when a goal is set towards achieving confidence, the client begins to understand what confidence is in terms of the common description you are using. All of the hours of discussion that follow, even the recollection of real-life experiences, are related to this common understanding. When the confidence goal is eventually met, it is only this described version of confidence that is achieved. The raw, spontaneous version of confidence has not been nourished because it has not been worked upon in its authentic state. This gain is therefore a type of act rather than a personal evolution.

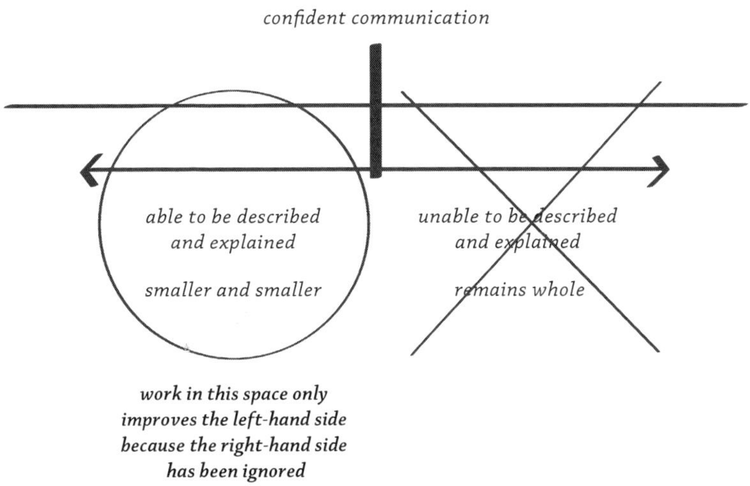

The client's confidence has been artificially boxed, analysed and returned to them. It has been worked on only in its describable state, and so describable improvement is the outcome.

The issue is amplified when confidence is broken down into smaller and smaller pieces, such as positive thinking and self-esteem. Not only are we putting these smaller descriptors into boxes that suffocate their real meaning in lived experience, but we are subdividing something already in a box (confidence) into other, smaller boxes and so further detaching it from its natural fluid state. We are not understanding the nature of confidence better. We are only understanding the nature of artificially-boxed confidence better. We are understanding the nature of raw, unexplainable confidence significantly worse.

You sit on the floor.

If you are unsure as to whether or not you have been working too much from the left-hand side of the line, look to your clients, students, athletes and children. If they have been left only with a series of techniques to deal with their original problem, then you have been working within the left-hand space, boxed in by describable concepts. If they have been genuinely lifted through their experience with you, and have not lost spontaneity when it comes to living with the resolution to their issue, then you have been able to find a balance between the two.

Other questions begin to appear around you.

- *As a teacher, are you aiming for a genuine, independent emotional uplift in your students as they learn with you, or have you replaced the expectation of uplift with a focus on holding discipline and whether or not your students demonstrate respect?*
- *As a parent, are you accepting the definitions that the school promotes of good and bad, right and wrong, and clever and not clever, or are you teaching your child the necessary attitude and skills to be able to win at the game of education while still remaining emotionally intact?*
- *As a coach, counsellor or therapist, do you look to your clients' describable outcomes as a marker for your success, or do you understand that if you are the best you can be then their best outcomes will be inevitable?*
- *Have you taken to blaming the pressures of your environment for your limitations or are you looking to improve your situation from within the limitations of your working environment?*

Know here and now that there *is* a way of superseding your restrictions, whether they arise from within or without. *Nine Rooms* has been constructed with the sole purpose of showing you how.

You may have been challenged in this room.

What would you like to do now?

Will you stay, leave or move on?

Please consider the story about the young monks
before making up your mind.

The Monks Who Went Blind

There were a group of young monks who took themselves off to live in the Wudang Mountains. One day, a single member of the group, while wandering alone close to a summit, stumbled across an entrance to a small cave. Near to the back, where the sunlight could not reach, he found an old scroll tucked into a corner. Excited, he left the cave, sat on a nearby rock, and unfurled the document. Enthralled, he read the best he could.

Eventually, as the sun went down, the monk wandered back to the group, parchment in hand, to share what he had found. The group were delighted to see him. He had been gone for so long! The young monk produced his scroll and, after rice and wild vegetables, green tea and prayers, they sat down together in the light of the fire to study the document.

The cleverest of the group was pleased to point out that the writing contained a short story about meditation – a practice these monks enjoyed every day. The text revealed that during meditation the initiate must 'gaze inward'. Roughly translated the scroll said: 'Little by little, day by day, turn your gaze further and further inwards until you can see within.' The monks were very impressed and, before settling down for the night, vowed to practice this technique to the letter.

In the days and months that followed the young monks proceeded to train themselves to turn their eyes 180 degrees in their sockets during meditation so that they could look inwards – towards the backs of their heads. It was harder than they had imagined, but they persisted until the skill was mastered. They did their best to ignore the excruciating headaches and blurred vision that now marred the simple beauty of their lives. They did not notice that they were no longer loving their meditative work.

Then, suddenly, one of the group went blind – the youngest monk. After the shock had died down, the friends met to discuss what to do next and, after careful consideration, decided that blindness was a gift of mastery of the art of this type of meditation. All of the monks hoped to go blind one day too.

A passing master arrived at the makeshift monastery and, after hearing their story, took pity on the youngsters. She sat them down and carefully, over many hours, explained to them the nature of meditation. She gave many examples about how its benefits were sensed, and how this sense bypassed the mind-body divide by treating it as one. She said that, during meditation, 'looking inwards' was a beautiful, indescribable feeling that was entirely personal; a feeling of oneness that came about naturally and grew uninhibited. It was a gift of beauty to you.

Sadly, for these young monks, the damage was done. With their vision impaired, they could no longer read the stories that would benefit them; stories that would enable them to grow complete rather than to be in pain. The master decided to stay with the young monks and to become their eyes. She read to them every night. In this way, they became enlightened, despite their tragic error of judgement. And the passing master found her light as a teacher of the partially sighted and the blind.

Time to open the next door.

Room Three

The room seems to be a meeting place.

There is a long table with chairs tucked under it.

On the table there is a sheet of white paper.

You walk towards the sheet of paper and pick it up. It reads:

"Your viewpoint has now been altered, again."

You turn the paper over. It contains an instruction:

"Move your positioning to the centre of the line."

You are now able to see both sides of the equation equally.

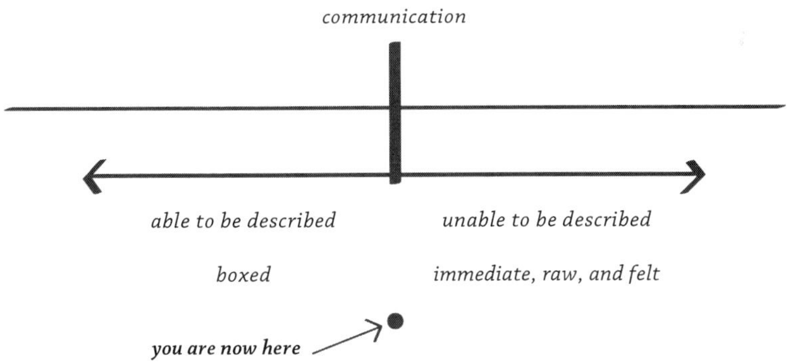

For your enlightenment appears the story of Ling.

Ling & Her Students

Ling, a music teacher, took a group of students to the Beijing Opera. The school's examination required them to analyse the performance of every role and to answer questions. Today it was the turn of the sheng. The group would go five times in total to study each major character in detail as it was being played. This visit was their first.

During the performance, the students noticed that some members of the audience were so enthralled by the player's interpretation of the sheng that they stood up and shouted, responding to special moments created by the player. They were so caught in the mood that they even 'ho oy oyed', especially at the longer unwavering notes the player so masterfully produced, alongside his superbly captivating movement.

Ling, as she often did, inwardly mourned for her students. She knew that they would never grow to experience the joy of the opera as fully as the generation before them. She knew that after the study was over her students would have analysed the players to death and so would not be able to experience opera spontaneously again. They would understand it technically and have knowledge to impress, but the life force of the play, the joy and the magic of the performance, would be lost to them, never to return. Education had killed the potential of a lifetime's experience of remarkable and spontaneous enjoyment.

From the story of Ling, you can begin to get a feel for both sides of the equation. In Ling's case, there is a realisation of the importance of the side of life that is 'felt' in the moment unanalysed. She also realises that the technical aspects of the opera (left hand, describable) are important for her students' examinations and therefore their academic futures. Ling does not know how to resolve the problem and feels restricted by the demands of the curriculum.

Ling's plight is one found throughout teaching, coaching and the caring professions where, as a concerned practitioner, you are only too aware of the limitations found within the expectations of your role.

You pause for a moment. You choose a chair and sit down.

You ponder on the following:

- *In the story, the teacher understands the destructive nature of what she is doing but continues to do it, year after year. She feels that, in the grand scheme of things, her students passing their examinations is more important than developing a love of opera. In parenting, coaching and the caring professions, the same type of situation often arises when we encourage our youngsters to conform 'for their own sakes'. It is a balancing act where we often feel we must tow the party line for the long-term benefit of the student or client. Consider examples of your own balancing act. What sorts of patterns emerge? What sort of denial supports these patterns?*

- ❖ *You can choose to change your perspective on these issues should you wish to do so, without rocking the boat. Advice will appear in the rooms that follow. How does that make you feel? Do you believe it yet? If not, why not?*

- ❖ *How often does your organisation promise training that will reach the right-hand side of the line when essentially it only reaches the left?*

Now, move your focus to the right-hand side of the line.

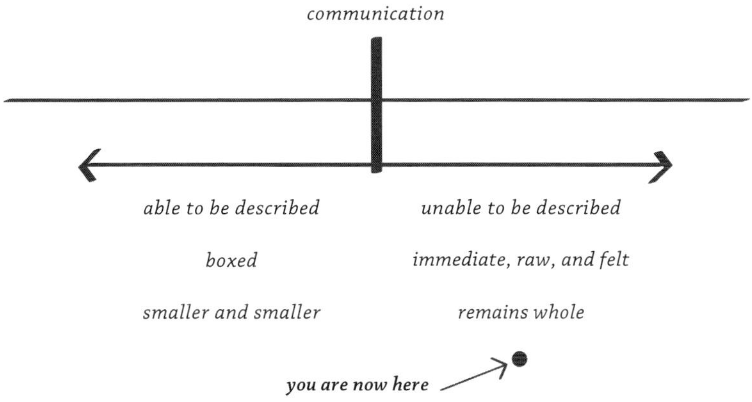

From your new viewpoint, the indescribable is prioritised over the describable. It is the place where immediacy and the reality of the individual reside. You are looking through the lens of someone who understands the potential of the indescribable. You are now on the side of the unexplainable and the mysterious.

A short dialogue becomes audible as if from outside of the room.

Student: Stop for a moment. 'Mysterious?' That doesn't sound very useful if I'm looking for answers.

Master: Many important answers are found where we are not used to looking.

Student: But does this mean the missing dimension won't be grounded?

Master: It will be entirely grounded. The indescribable, the mysterious, is a place where most of what is grounded resides.

Student: That makes no sense.

Master: Sometimes we have to challenge the fundamentals of what we believe in order to make progress.

As we have discussed, if something is indescribable and we describe it, it becomes something entirely different – described. In moving from one side of the line to the other, its character is entirely changed. Take an unsolved crime being solved or a mystery unravelled. If something is moved from one side to the other it becomes not only changed but the exact opposite of what it was. The implication is therefore that the describable and the indescribable must stay on their own sides of the line if they are to remain their authentic selves. They can work together, side by side, but they cannot move from their places. Their worlds are set.

If we look to our story about Ling and the opera, we can see that, for the opera audience, not knowing too much about the technical side of the performance can enhance the pleasure of the experience. It introduces the potential for genuine and grounded enjoyment because of the element of mystery it contains for them. It becomes a type of magical environment where they enter the mysterious space of the theatre and experience the story and the music fully and as one in the moment. Their intellect does not interfere.

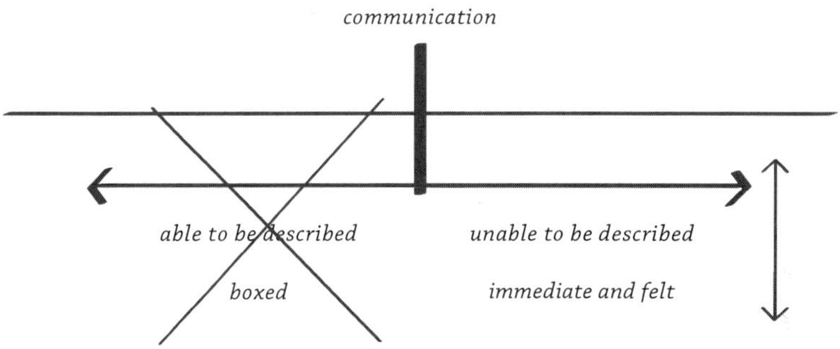

From the diagram you can see that for the opera audience the right-hand side, the indescribable, seems to be conversing with itself. The indescribable nature of the event, in this case the performances of the players, inspires the indescribable nature of the audience's raw emotion to come about. The right side of the line in the play is communicating immediately with the right side of the line in the audience's individual experience. The technical, describable side of the line has been bypassed altogether.

In this way, indescribability is not a difficulty, a problem or a fault. It is a quality. When feelings, so obviously in existence (because they are felt by us) can only be authentically described as indescribable, it means that they are likely to be of more value to us in their undescribed state than when described. Indescribability does not have to be an invitation to solve the puzzle. We can, instead, celebrate the value and the feeling of indescribability: the joy of its mysteriousness.

You see a scroll placed at the other end of the table. You go to it and unroll it. It contains a question:

"When did you last celebrate the mystery of a problem with your clients or students, before rushing ahead to sort it out?"

We are nearing the place in which our missing dimension is known to exist. As we approach, it may be prudent to mention that, although personal, the missing dimension does not require you to live your life in an entirely different way. It does not require you to be openly emotional. It does not require you to express what you are thinking at all times. It does not require you to openly disagree with people at work. And it certainly does not require you to aim for some kind of guru status in order to affect change. Instead you understand the importance of boxed approaches to your profession and your responsibilities to tick these boxes. You understand the value of repeatability. You understand the importance of working within the traditional parameters of your vocation without inhibiting or devaluing its nature.

A final ponderance before moving on:

- *How is it possible to explore something so intrinsically of the moment and personal as the right-hand side of the line without altering its nature?*

Here are nine suggested answers, a few of which you have already experienced in the first three rooms. All of these ideas inspire 'unboxed' and individual responses.

- *First, you describe the indescribable simply by calling it 'indescribable'.*

- *Second, you enjoy 'indescribability' as a valuable and complete description rather than a challenge, a problem or a fault.*

- *Third, you open yourself up to the possibility of unlabelled emotional responses being evoked. Instead of labelling how you feel, you simply remain open to the feeling's rise and fall. These responses are therefore in the moment, particular to you and are not compartmentalised.*

- *Fourth, you use real-world examples to evoke responses. Familiarity can enable individual response. We all have different histories and therefore react to things in different ways. For example, a description of an annoying colleague could conjure up an individual response by reminding you of when you were in a similar situation.*

- *Fifth, you continue to work creatively through storytelling and the use of metaphor. Creativity provokes spontaneous individual responses.*

- *Sixth, you continue to ask questions, the answers to which are entirely the reader's own.*

- *Seventh, you describe things by the absence of their qualities – by what they are not. Here you are left to fill in the gaps for yourself as to what they are, so you are not boxed in by artificial definitions. For example, if an environment is described as containing the complete absence of hate, you can start to get a feel for what that environment means to you personally. It is not a description of what is, it is a description of what is not. Watch out too for the double negative: 'This cannot not be the case', designed to stop you in your tracks and push you further towards an individual reaction.*

- *Eighth, you do not explore what something is. Instead, you explore what something does. Rather than explore what the missing dimension is we explore the effect it has on us from the right-hand side of the line.*

- *Ninth, and perhaps most important, you submit to the limitations of the medium of writing and welcome them with open arms. Words, even when used to inspire individual responses, are still limiting.*

The guidelines will often need to be broken but, hopefully, as you pass through the rooms, enough authenticity will remain for you to gain your own understanding of the missing dimension and what it can do for you, your clients and your students.

By the way, we have arrived.

A bit of a warning.

Before we proceed, you may have guessed that the missing dimension is not a philosophical or psychological space. It thrives absolutely within the immediacy of your reality. There is no safety net – none whatsoever. It is very, very personal.

The learning contained here, once known, is very difficult to unknow without a great deal of targeted denial.

You cannot say you have not been warned.

Of course, some mysteries are irresistible.

The Middle Chambers

As you travel to the next room,
please consider *Pedro in China*.

Pedro in China

Pedro's understanding of meditation came from sitting with a master for a year on a mountain in China. Beforehand he had studied meditation in Madrid for quite some time and thought he knew the art form well. Pedro could sometimes still his mind for up to an hour at a time before his thoughts came visiting.

In China Pedro learnt that he had misunderstood the fundamentals – the basics of the form. Mediation had nothing to do with stilling the mind to access the depth. This way of looking at things only created a strange and artificial state, at best, that was hard to maintain. Instead, with the help of the master, Pedro learnt to access a place where there was no mind-body divide at all. Everything was naturally stilled as one. In doing so, his meditation was assured to always be in the moment.

The master said the following: 'Where are your thoughts?' Pedro would point to his head. 'You feel them there because you have come to know they originate there?

Right?' Pedro would nod. 'If I had been your teacher for many years and told you that your mind was in your right toe, and you believed me, where do you think you would feel your thoughts?' Pedro would point to his right toe. 'Where we place the origin of our monkey mind is therefore a choice. You can choose to place it here, here, or far, far away.'

Pedro was told to first place his mind in different parts of his body and to focus on where his mind was each time. This exercise he did for a month. Next, he was told to place the mind in the whole of his body, to feel it as one unit. This Pedro did for two months. Pedro then spent the next three months placing the mind in places outside of the body, in front of him in the air, or on a nearby chair. Four months were spent with the mind permeating the entire environment, everywhere all around, at the same time. Finally, five months were spent with the mind permeating the environment together with Pedro's body, all as one.

Pedro learnt that the mind-body divide would vanish because it was an invention. Mindlessness would replace mindfulness, and only then could it lead to the extreme wellbeing of the meditative state. Pedro had felt nothing like it. Sometimes he would need to be brought out of mediation after many hours of sitting. The master said, 'In everyday life, the function of the mind and the body is to work as one unit. The same is true when you are meditating.'

You can understand the potential of a seed by
planting it in good soil and nurturing it as it grows.

Room Four

A square room with large windows along one side
and desks in crooked lines.

It looks like a classroom that has been abandoned.

There is a large chalkboard at the front.

On the board has been written:

> *"Welcome to your exploration of the Complete Transmission Experience – or CTE for short."*

The Complete Transmission Experience is the name I have given to the missing dimension. It sits firmly on the right-hand side of the line and, in doing so, engages you in the individual realities of your students and clients.

A message appears as if scribbled on the board:

> *"Things might not be how they originally appear."*

Consider the scenario of the group affected by a single person.

The Group Affected by a Single Person

You are a calm person. You are in a room with others who are similar – calm. Together you create a calm atmosphere, a calm environment.

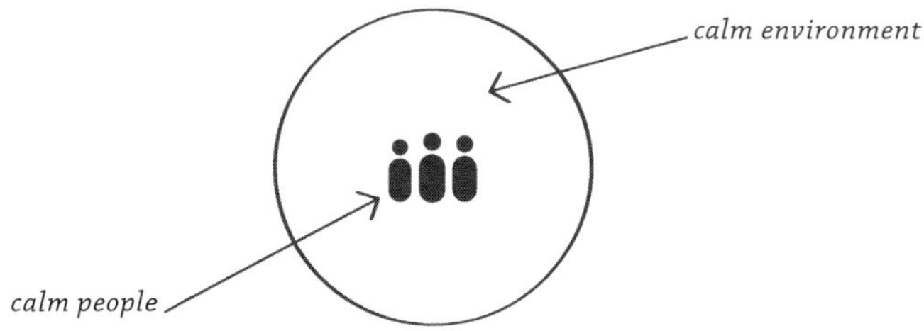

The room is an easy place to be.

Enter a volatile member of your team. We will call him Gordon Xi. Yesterday, Gordon Xi was his usual angry and reactive self, which came to a head when he exploded in a meeting. Today he is trying to put on a front of stability. Despite Gordon's act, the atmosphere in the room changes as soon as he arrives. Everybody in the group is alert to his potentially unpredictable behaviour and this reaction creates tension. You are each affected in your own ways.

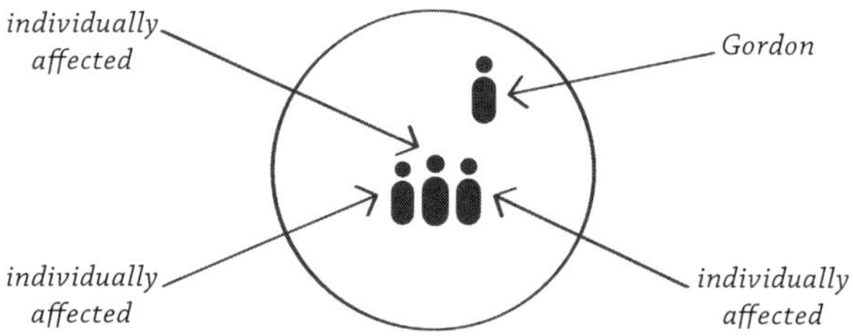

Gordon, via the Complete Transmission Experience, has affected the room.

Here is another way of looking at the situation:

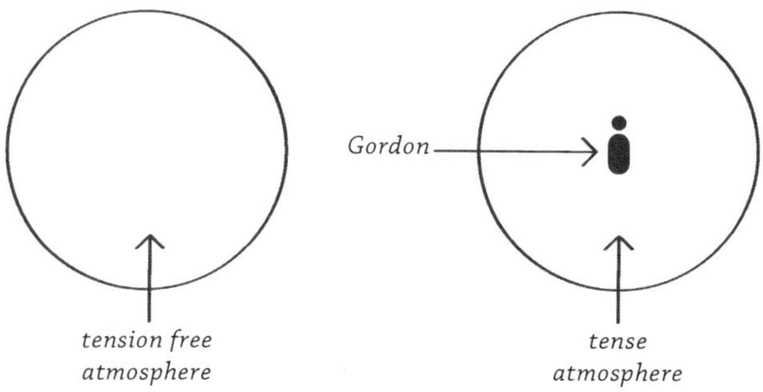

Gordon, via the CTE, has affected those in the vicinity, and a tense atmosphere has come about. Gordon's volatility is stronger, more certain and more dominating than the calmness of the other people in the room, and so it emotionally alters them as individuals, instantly. The feel of the room changes because the emotional state of the people in the room changes. Before Gordon came into the room, you and the others were being a certain way and so the environment reflected this way of being. Gordon came into the environment and impacted all of the people in it, and so the feel of the environment changed.

When interpreting what has happened to the room there may be a temptation to jump towards a description based on the science of human behaviour: 'Yes, psychology suggests that the group's reaction is caused by...', or, 'I know, sociology explains this interaction by...', or, 'This anthropologist says that body language can be so subtle that...'. However, these interpretations emerge from the left-hand side of the line, a place where there is the opportunity to describe things in more and more detail, to be objective and analytical. What about the same scenario expressed from the right-hand side of the line? What does it look like in terms of immediacy and lived experience? What is happening there?

You are invited to consider the story of the flower.

The Story of the Flower

There was once a bright yellow flower in a field. It emitted a subtle but glorious scent. Bees were attracted to it and people would come towards it to experience its beauty. Children liked to say 'This flower makes me feel happy', or words to that effect, and they would move on a little more lifted than before. A sage and his young ward overheard these comments. 'What do you think?' asked the sage. The young ward smiled. He knew of this question from conversations before and had an answer prepared. 'People say that the flower makes them feel happy,' he replied, 'but this cannot be the case.' 'Why is that?' asked the sage. The ward beamed, 'Because the flower is not doing anything other than being a flower. It cannot do anything to anyone. It cannot make anyone feel anything.' 'And?' encouraged the sage. 'Therefore,' continued the ward, 'the people are being uplifted by how the flower is, not by what the flower does.'

From the right-hand side our CTE can best be described as us being who we are, and how this 'beingness' affects the people around us. In our scenario, Gordon's right-hand side of the line is directly communicating with the right-hand side of everyone else's lines, affecting them, and, in turn, changing the feel of the environment.

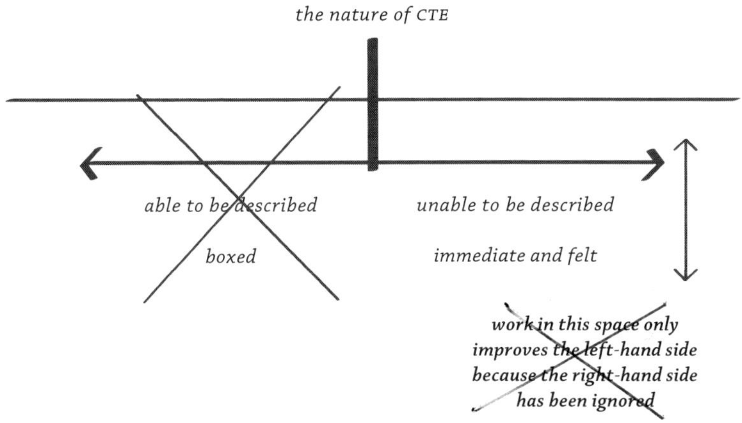

It is an enormous concept with vast implication.

You pause to reread and consider.

You look back to the board. The old information has been erased and a new exercise has appeared.

1. *Choose four objects that are quite close together. If you are in a park, you might select a tree, a patch of grass, a path and a piece of litter. If you are in a room, you might select a cup, a pen, a computer and a printer.*

2. *Look at the objects one by one. Spend time with each. Do not name these objects. Do not name any part of them. Do not compare them. Do not contrast them. Do not be a student at school. Simply let them be as you watch and become involved. There is no struggle because you don't have to do anything other than look. It's the easiest thing in the world to do. It's what we did before we knew of words. Don't battle yourself. Don't do this or that. It would serve no purpose whatsoever. Simply free yourself of the need to label and describe. That's all there is.*

3. *Repeat the observations in different locations.*

4. *How did it feel to glimpse the experience of the right-hand side of the line?*

You return to the flower.

Important to our understanding of the CTE is that the flower is not *intentionally* transmitting anything. Flowers can't do that. As the young ward says, 'The flower cannot *do* anything to anyone. It cannot *make* anyone feel anything.' Instead, it is simply *being* and, in doing so, is causing a reaction around it. Another way of looking at it is that the flower is *being* transmitted.

When we translate this experience to Gordon, we find the original situation becoming a little clearer. Gordon, just by being Gordon, Gordon undescribed, Gordon in the broadest possible sense, is affecting the environment. From the right-hand side of the line, it is not what Gordon is *doing* (this would be describable) that is causing the effect, it is who Gordon is *being* (that is indescribable) that is so profoundly affecting the people around him.

It may be an inconvenient truth, but the Complete Transmission Experience is something that happens moment to moment, continuously, regardless. It is not something we can choose to manufacture or an action we can decide to take. It is something that is somehow instantly done. It is a type of natural law. Everything about us, on every level, is being transmitted continuously.

A message appears:

"Please prepare yourself."

You stand and move to the window.

There is absolutely nowhere for you to hide.

The Complete Transmission Experience
is the unspoken core of communication.

The CTE cannot not happen.

You pause.

You: ‘What?’ (again).

After a while you realise you need an example. Questions form in your mind. 'What damage might my CTE be causing to the people around me?' And, more importantly, 'How do I fix it?'

Here is your example.

Tension is a major inhibiting factor when it comes to your CTE. Healthy tension, such as that which keeps our body upright or causes the rush of adrenaline and nervousness that you feel before an interview or an exam, can keep you strong and vibrant, inspired and challenged. We are talking about the tension that inhibits and disables body and mind – tension that restricts rather than enables.

If you hold restrictive tension this will instantly create the feel of a restrictive environment via your CTE, and so negatively impact your students or clients. It will permeate all that you do with them. It cannot *not* contradict any good you are doing. The negative tension you might be holding, whether you know about it or not, *will* be transmitted and restrict those around you. Your CTE transmits the whole picture of who you are, instantly and continuously.

If you are unsure whether or not you are holding tension, ponder over the following:

- *How exhausted are you at the end of the day? Tension free people are rarely exhausted by their job, no matter how busy.*
- *How often do you laugh at work – a proper relaxed laugh, rather than a forced or shallow one? How often do you even smile a genuine smile? How often do you silently judge others who laugh and smile? Tension free people are often genuinely happy people.*
- *Do you need to draw a line between home and work? Tension free people rarely need to do this as they don't need to 'escape' the tension of their job.*

As we have said, we are aiming for the type of freedom from tension that enables an athlete to run faster or enables you to multitask with ease despite the pressures of your environment. It isn't an absence of drive and purpose. Instead the lack of tension allows you to function at a much higher level. If you can succeed in genuinely releasing some of your tension, then your CTE will be of someone truly more relaxed, and this will be transmitted to those around you. If, however, you only succeed in *pretending* to be tension free, or mimicking the body language or tone of voice of being tension free, (a swan that is calm on the surface but paddling furiously underneath the surface, against the current) then your CTE will transmit the whole picture: the pretence of someone being tension free. Your CTE cannot *not* present the whole picture. It is authenticity personified.

How to resolve the tension situation

Tension seems to hide everywhere; most noticeably within the expectation of our roles. Indeed, sometimes, if we are not holding tension, it can be perceived that we do not care about our job. Here are some exercises designed to alleviate tension. They may not be what you are expecting as, on the whole, they educate experientially. They will be developed as you pass through the rooms. If you can gradually release your tension in real terms, you are taking your first steps to improving your CTE.

Tension-Releasing Exercises: Level One

- *Put yourself in the vicinity of those who hold tension. Sit next to them. Talk to them. See how you feel. Under no circumstances label your feelings. Do not judge the people you are with. This exercise is all about your unlabelled, felt response – nothing else. How do these people, as individuals, make you feel moment to moment? Do you want to stay there or leave?*

- *Notice as you are doing the exercise that you are not actually feeling the tension each person holds, rather you are feeling the person who holds the tension. Had you realised that before?*

- *Repeat the exercise but this time sit next to someone who does not hold unnecessary tension. How do these people as individuals make you feel moment to moment? Do you want to stay there or leave?*

- *Now prepare yourself for a difficult question. Perhaps it is one you are hoping to avoid: Which type of person do you think your students, clients or team would prefer to be with day after day and week after week? Would they prefer to be with those ignorant of their tension or those working to alleviate it?*

Your CTE matters.

✳

Time to move on.

As you travel to the next room, please read
One Child, Three Stories, Three Endings.

One Child, Three Stories, Three Endings

Story One

There were once two parents and their single child who they loved with their lives – Billy. There was one problem. Billy could not sit still. When Billy's school sent a report home saying that he couldn't concentrate and, most importantly, he was distracting the other children, they became concerned. 'Perhaps,' the school suggested, 'Billy should be tested.' Billy's parents, being the loving people they were, wanted the best for him and so they took him to a doctor. When they were told that he had a particular condition and that there were drugs that could calm him down, they quickly agreed he should take them. The school were happy because his behaviour improved. Billy's parents were happy because (despite his dulled state that sometimes worried them) he was able to take some examinations and go to college. The school told Billy's parents he had 'achieved his potential'.

Story Two

There were once two parents and their single child who they loved with their lives – Billy. There was one problem. Billy could not sit still. Billy's school sent a report home saying that he couldn't concentrate and, most importantly, he was distracting the other children and preventing them from learning. 'Perhaps,' they suggested, 'Billy should be tested.' Being the loving parents they were, they took Billy to a doctor who confirmed that he had a certain condition. The doctor explained to them that there were drugs that could help, but first she wanted to try something else. 'Had they thought of sport?' The doctor said that some very successful gymnasts had similar conditions to Billy's and maybe they might try that first. Being the parents they were, they took him to a local gymnastic club. Billy was very enthusiastic. He ran around trying everything. He was a happy lad. The lead coach approached Billy's parents. 'I'm afraid he doesn't have the self-discipline for gymnastics,' she said, 'it becomes dangerous to be reckless in a gym.' Billy's parents took him back to the doctor who said, 'Well, at least we tried gymnastics,' and she prescribed him his medication. Billy's parents were happy because (despite his dulled state that worried them) he was able to take some examinations and go to college. The school told Billy's parents he had 'achieved his potential'.

Story Three

There were once two parents and their single child who they loved with their lives – Billy. There was one problem. Billy could not sit still. Billy's school sent a report home saying that he couldn't concentrate and, most importantly, he was distracting the other children from learning. 'Perhaps,' they suggested, 'Billy should be tested.' Being the loving parents they were, they took Billy to a doctor who confirmed that Billy had a condition. The doctor explained that there were drugs that could help but that something else could be tried. She said that some very successful gymnasts had Billy's condition and maybe he should give sport a go first. Being the parents they were, they took Billy to a local gymnastic club. He was very enthusiastic and ran around trying everything. He was a happy lad. The lead coach approached Billy's parents. 'He has potential,' she said, 'but he will have to have a different sort of training program.' Dedicated to helping him, they agreed. It meant a lot of commitment from Billy's dad who had to drive him around, and a lot of time from his mum who had to find an extra job to pay for the program, but they were happy to do so. To start with Billy's training involved him jogging around the gym until he was exhausted. When he could hardly breathe, hardly move, he was taught his gymnastics. Often, when Billy was running around, the lead coach would join him for a lap or two, saying nothing, sometimes talking about this and that. Billy loved these moments in particular – he had no idea why. The lead coach was a strong, calm, certain and no-nonsense individual and took it upon herself to employ coaches with the potential to be the same. They became stronger, calmer and more certain coaches under her guidance. This approach meant that the club could work as a barrier to the bullying culture that permeated the sport higher up. Billy's gymnastic environment was therefore supportive of him. As Billy's talent grew, more of his energy could be put into his gymnastic training, and he was required to run less and less. Through his teenage years there were struggles and at one point he was banned from the gym for a month only to return more determined than ever. Ten years later Billy found himself part of his national team and two years after that he was at the Olympic Games. An hour before his first event, Billy, for no particular reason, found himself visited by a rush of extreme and uncontrollable energy. The coach saw Billy's state and called him over. Together they went to the warmup gym at the back of the arena and ran around it. For most of the time the coach was silent, and only on occasion spoke of something or other. Billy won a silver medal. His parents were the happiest any parents could be and his school boasted about him for years to come. 'He achieved his potential,' they said.

The indefinable quality of who you are can inspire.

Room Five

The room is L-shaped and you cannot see what
is around the corner.

There is a hint of colour on the walls, mainly yellow.

Old wooden floors, once stained white, support
an intricately-woven mat on the floor.

Consider this situation.

The Group Help Educate a Single Person

A group of strong, calm and centred individuals are in a room. In walks somebody known to be a complainer. She proceeds to complain about her day, the workload, the boss, the pressure of her deadlines and the lack of time. It is a way she has learnt to be, and daily she seeks ways to reinforce her investment. Many organisations have such individuals. You may have experienced one or two yourself. They work on the principle that it is easier to moan about a situation than it is to find a workable way to put it right. This time, the group of calm people in the room, as part of their role, see themselves as informal educators. They understand the nature of the connection between their individual Complete Transmission Experiences and the people they are informally educating. As the complainer continues to complain, the group remain natural and unaffected. It is something they have practised, because they understand its fundamental value. Together their calmness is deeper, broader, stronger and more certain than the complainer's way of being and so the environment remains unaffected by the complainer's well-practised interruption. The group are not pretending in order to achieve their ends. It is simply who they are – strong and calm people. They do not seek to be drawn into a battle.

They do not seek to block out the complainer. They do not look to argue. Instead, they simply allow themselves to remain strong and centred, and for the complainer to continue to be as she is. When she asks them their opinion on a contentious matter, they answer kindly, neither agreeing nor disagreeing. They make tea and offer her some. Very quickly the complainer finds she cannot continue her rant because the environment is not conducive to complainers. Even though she has not been contained, constrained or confronted, she calms down and joins the group, starting to engage in other topics of conversation. She has felt the calmness of the environment created by the other three people in the room and has been affected by it.

The effect has taken very little effort from the group because calmness is simply who they are as people. Previously the group did not have success like this because their strength and calmness were less than genuinely felt by them. They decided to improve themselves in this area as individuals (something covered later on in the Nine Rooms), and in doing so, their individual CTEs were automatically improved too. As we know, the Complete Transmission Experience happens whether we like it or not, and this time the group chose to make theirs as helpful and as nourishing as possible.

Now imagine a school or university where absolutely all staff are strong, calm, vibrant and centred in their own individual ways, whether they are leading, teaching, preparing food, cleaning or grounds keeping. Wouldn't most students placed in this environment for years be unavoidably strengthened, lifted and educated by the atmosphere they were surrounded by? How could the CTE of this environment not affect most of them in a nourishing way? Wouldn't they be able to learn their lessons far more effectively? Wouldn't far less time be wasted on discipline because the issues would be less likely to arise in the first place? Wouldn't a focus on wellbeing be intrinsic to the learning environment because the teachers would be genuinely being well rather than focusing on 'wellbeing' in a box? Wouldn't the students enjoy school more because of the consistency of the environment? Wouldn't this enjoyment mean better attendance and better results? Wouldn't new teachers coming into this environment be likely to develop the same sort of attitude because they would be experiencing the CTE of all the others? Wouldn't all of this change be possible without having to alter one iota of the curriculum or challenging government intervention? Wouldn't a stronger, more authentic curriculum eventually be created from this perspective because those affected would eventually rise to the top and therefore be able to make these sorts of decisions? If a school's value statement (such as 'stronger, wiser, braver') was personified by everyone, wouldn't these values permeate the very fabric of the organisation via the staffs' CTE? Wouldn't most schools be very, very different places? Wouldn't there be absolutely no downside to this approach?

If, instead, the teachers in this school choose to become frustrated, reactive and tense as, for example, they are forced to incorporate constantly narrowing government incentives, they also choose to allow this frustration to be communicated via their CTE. Even if they try to hide their frustration, their CTE contains the quality of 'someone trying to hide frustration' because the whole picture is transmitted. On the other hand, should they realise the importance of choosing to remain genuinely strong, calm and tension free as they incorporate these ineffective and prohibitive 'incentives', their CTE will be nourishing to the students rather than disabling to them. The children are much less likely to feel emotionally restricted or restrained due to the government's impositions if the people around them have learnt not to be emotionally affected by them also.

Take, for example, something we are often encouraged to believe through our training in coaching, teaching, leadership and counselling: that we need to develop a front to protect ourselves.

Via the CTE, the whole of who we are is being transmitted. There can be no parts separated from the whole. So, when we put on a front, what we are actually doing is this:

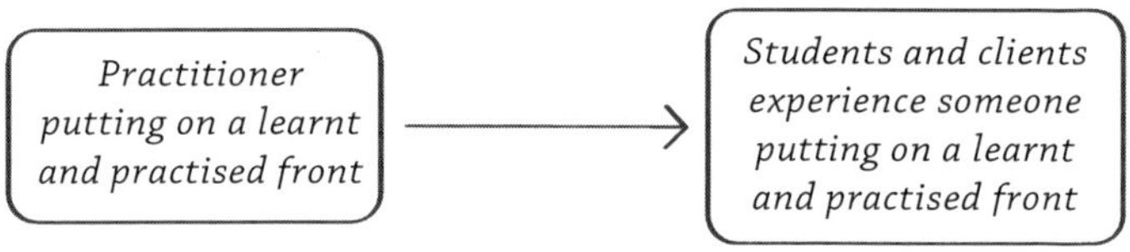

If what is presented to your students or clients, day after day, includes the feeling of somebody putting on a front, it means you are pretending to be someone you are not. This contradiction, via your CTE, undermines the feel of anything authentic you are trying to achieve.

Take an example from the world of counselling. Imagine you are a counsellor who believes that a professional stance equates to putting on a professional front – being careful not to expose anything of yourself to your clients, except on the odd occasion when you feel something appropriate can be revealed. You fear, as some counsellors do, that if you don't hide the 'real you' by projecting a stereotypical image, you will make yourself vulnerable to the client, maybe even that your counselling will become more about you than them.

What you might believe you are doing is this:

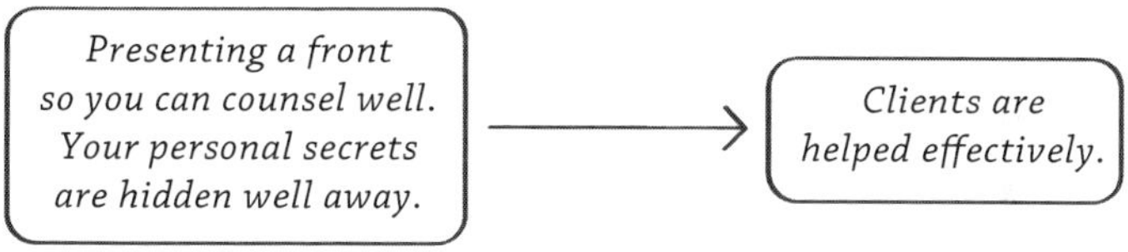

After all, it can be quite a minefield out there. But, something very different is happening in terms of your CTE.

What you are actually doing is this:

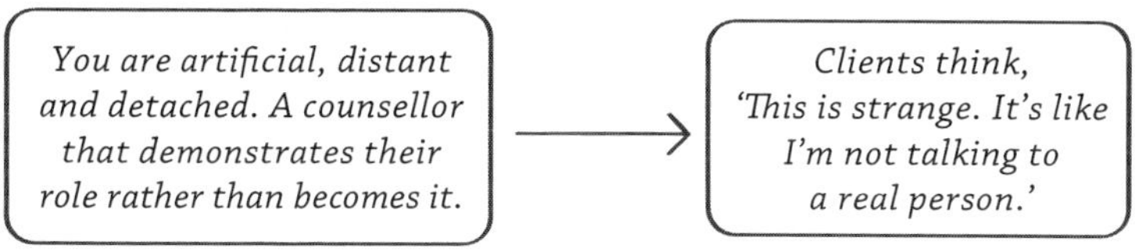

Because of the nature of the CTE, the counsellor who is pretending actively inhibits those they are trying to help, and the effects quickly manifest as problems.

For example, in teaching, holding classroom discipline while putting on a front will become a time-consuming affair, a contrived effort. The teacher will blame class after class, year after year, for their misbehaviour. The opposite is a teacher who does not put on a front. They *become* the role rather than *pretend* the role and, perhaps after a difficult start, will eventually have better discipline because they develop a more authentic sense of communication with the class. In counselling and teaching, there might be a concern that the practitioner will be indiscrete if they are not putting on a front. Perhaps they might worry about being overly friendly or accidently overstepping professional boundaries. However, when we are *being* the role as opposed to *demonstrating* the role we are still the consummate professional, perhaps even more so because the protocols have become intrinsically part of who we are in that situation. We *are* a professional rather than *pretending* to be a professional. The only difference is that we are not hiding away. When we find this place, our CTE does not contradict the authenticity of what we are trying to achieve for our students or clients.

You are advised to pause for a moment.

You sit down on the mat to think.

A question appears.

"How do you train somebody to 'become' the role rather than to 'pretend' the role?"

Imagine these two scenarios.

A teacher, Adrian, who cannot hold discipline particularly well, is advised to observe another that does. Adrian notes down every detail of what the other does to the finest of points. He then goes on to apply these observations to his own classes, with mediocre results. He says that these techniques do not work for him and so searches out other methods, but these only produce the same kind of tepid results time and time again.

A different teacher, Victoria, who also cannot hold discipline particularly well, observes the same teacher as Adrian. Similarly, she notes down every detail of what the teacher does. But there is something else. She spends time getting the feel for how the teacher is being in the classroom and the sense of momentum and expectation she creates. Victoria realises that the feel of the environment is key to the disciplinary techniques being effective and that it is her responsibility as the teacher to create this feel. With this in mind, she asks if she might co-teach with the expert teacher. By doing so, she begins to get into the swing of things.

Afterwards, when Victoria begins to work with her own classes, her results are initially haphazard. But, as her understanding of her personal responsibility for the classroom environment grows, so does her level of discipline. Eventually she becomes a teacher who other teachers observe, because she understands that holding discipline is so much more than technique alone.

Take an example from a coaching perspective.

A wellbeing coach, Anthony, is working at a university. He is responsible for the wellbeing of everyone on the campus. It's a busy job. 'I'm having to rush around and do so much,' he says, as he darts from one part of the university to the other, obviously stressed. Clearly, Anthony feels he is doing well because he always manages to hide his stress from his clients. 'I get to help a lot of people in a day,' he says.

Here we have a wellbeing coach who is not living his creed. His CTE reveals that he is only pretending to be stress free. He is 'demonstrating' the wellbeing he is trying to coach in others, but underneath he does not genuinely have it. When he uses his wellbeing techniques with his clients the results can only be limited because his CTE contradicts what he is trying to achieve. It is far better for a coach to tell the client they are tense rather than to try to hide it. The coach will come across as truthful rather than artificial and most importantly, human. Of course, if the coach knows to stay genuinely calm, centred and tension free, despite the pressures of the job (as many coaches do), then the outcome will be entirely different. An authentic coach and a more authentically-nourished client.

When you put on a front something else happens too. There is an automatic disconnect between your front and your genuine emotions. Imagine being in front of a teacher, coach, leader or counsellor for hundreds of hours who has no connection with genuine happiness. They may act it out and demonstrate the body language and facial expressions associated with it, when appropriate, but they do not feel it. If you were a youngster, what might you learn about the nature of feelings via the CTE of your teachers in this environment? How many schools, coaching and counselling establishments and leadership courses discourage the feeling or expression of joy? How often is happiness irradicated in a quest for 'perfection'? How often are artificial environments labelled 'excellent', put on a pedestal and then paraded as a model of 'what our institutions should be aiming for'?

You and your CTE are the same thing.

Your CTE cannot *not* be you.

You walk to the end of the room and peer around the corner. Here you find your next set of tension-releasing exercises, previously hidden. They will help you to further alleviate your tension and to improve your awareness of its destructive effects.

Tension-Releasing Exercises: Level Two

As mentioned before, holding onto unhealthy levels of tension as a way of being might well be the most fundamentally destructive experience our CTE can transmit. Tension spreads like a virus. It limits thinking and prohibits creativity. It blinds us to the bigger picture. Tension limits our emotions to only those linked to fight or flight: fear, anger, aggression or anxiety. In these states we are unable to feel genuine happiness; the brain will not allow it.

We have already increased our awareness of tension by noticing the effect others (who hold tension and who don't) have on us. Now we move to an improved awareness of ourselves. Here, similar to before, it is very much about noticing how we feel; again, without naming that feeling. The trick at this stage is not to seek to alter anything at all about yourself but simply to notice. Become aware when tension arises, let the associated emotions occur, feel them fully, let them pass, then let this awareness go. Forget it. Nothing else. Easy as that.

- *Notice throughout the working day where your tension trigger points are. Focus on how you feel when the actual trigger is happening.*
- *Sit with the feeling. Do not name it. Do not judge it.*
- *Repeat as often as you can.*
- *Repeat some more.*

Time to move on to the next room.

Consider *The Problem with Posterity* on your way.

The Problem with Posterity

There was an elderly Taoist master of ninety-four. She was a master of the movement art called chi gong. In fact, she had mastered the energetic side of her craft so entirely that her hair, a long time white, had turned almost entirely back to black.

Sometimes, the master would be visited by students who would sit with her respectfully, work alongside her and leave her company more aware than before they came. However, on one occasion this was not the case. A group of chi gong teachers from outside of the master's culture sought her out. They knocked at the door of her very ordinary little house with a very special translator in tow. You see, they wanted to understand everything about her methods perfectly.

After partaking of tea, the group explained to the master that they wanted to improve their own teaching by asking her questions and watching her work. The master of course agreed because it is the duty of a master to educate when they can. Then the recording equipment came out. An hour or two passed during which time the master was asked pre-prepared questions and her chi gong sequence was filmed. The group asked her to repeat it three times so that they could look at it again and again from different angles. The group left delighted with their accomplishment. One even said, 'We will keep this for posterity. It will not be lost.'

It is extremely bad manners to film a master at work. They will never complain because they are polite, but you may need to remember this fact for future reference. Also, what you film will hold absolutely nothing of value. It will be worthless. The group of teachers chose to record the master 'for posterity' so that they could analyse her answers and copy her chi gong sequences in detail. They wanted to keep the footage for generations to come. They did not know that this is not the meaning of posterity.

The group had a wonderful, once-in-a-lifetime opportunity to work alongside a master; something that would have enabled significant personal growth in them all. This personal expansion would have then been passed on to their students via their transmission and to their students and to their students. This is the true meaning of 'for posterity'. Instead, this opportunity was lost forever because of the group's concern for narrow, artificial and two-dimensional memory. They could only achieve, at best, artificial growth.

Room Six

A bright room with an open feel.

It's quiet and still.

The natural light feels calming.

A Single Person Educates the Group

Imagine: a group of disgruntled workers are in a room waiting to meet their new boss. They used to like to pull the wool over the eyes of their previous manager and are waiting to see whether they might be able do the same thing here. In walks someone with the feel of a naturally strong, centred and balanced individual. She sits, introduces herself and begins to explain to them, extremely clearly, her expectations and the new levels of accountability she will be putting in place. She outlines the type of thing that will result in them being promoted and the type of thing that will result in them being dismissed. She is not acting. She doesn't need to pretend because she is the total embodiment of a confident, proficient, natural leader. There is no gap between who she is and what she does.

The group do not necessarily like what they hear from their boss, but her CTE means that almost everyone finds themselves respecting her. Despite there being no aggression, no threat and no introduction of conflict on her part, she has marked her authority simply by being the real deal. In fact, one or two of the group are reminded of a single politician whose strong and steady demeanour exposed an entire bumbling government. Some of them reflect on the meeting and compare her to their previous boss who would say the same sort of things but with a forced, artificial and sometimes defensive attitude. He seemed to think that entertaining them at Christmas and flattering their egos would bring them on side, regardless of what they had to put up with for the rest of the year. Behind his back they would laugh at his transparency and take advantage of it. Many of the group have the feeling that there will be no need for manipulation or tricks with the new boss. Over the weeks and months that follow, the working environment is lifted and wellbeing is improved along with the workers' sense of loyalty, without there once being a need to discuss 'lift' or 'wellbeing', or even to mention 'loyalty'.

You have a choice whether to develop your CTE (and so naturally lift and empower people) or to deny the existence of your CTE (and leave the results to chance). We are the creators of our environment on a more immediate and personal level than we may have ever imagined because the environment we create is a representation of who we are. Who we are being *is* our environment, and if who we are being has merged with our skills without superficiality or artifice, then the environment we create will become authentically and seamlessly ours to lift.

A thought appears. You say aloud: *'How do I raise my CTE?'*

Someone replies: *'The answer is in the next room. Remember not to rush ahead.'*

A Story About Four Head Teachers

There was once a head teacher, Moira, who prided herself in attracting the most accomplished teachers to her school. She spent a lot of money on advertising. The problem was that turnover of staff was high, and she could not understand why. On one occasion, she employed two of the most experienced deputy heads in the country, both of whom had excellent references and were known to be resilient and able to stand on their own two feet. Within a year, both deputies seemed unable to do anything well. They could not even seem to manage the simplest of decisions. 'Their references must have been lies,' thought the head. This was a thought she often had with the many members of staff who seemed to show promise but ultimately failed her. Both deputies left the school quickly and went on to become major successes. In fact, both eventually became excellent head teachers themselves. Of course, this particular head never once considered that she was the root of the problem with staff retention. Was it a coincidence that there was absolutely no joy in this school (other than from students who rebelled against the suffocating environment before being instantly expelled, or from the staff who frequently laughed at Moira behind her back in order to stay sane)? Was it a coincidence that not one student or member of staff in the school was ever once inspired by her?

There was another head teacher, Patrick, who was renowned for turning failing schools around. He would march in, spend two years telling people what to do, and leave with results radically improved. He was so good at his job that he won an award for his efforts. Well done him! This head did not think much of the word 'inspiring' – he relied on manipulation and bullying. His CTE was incredibly direct and cutting, as are the CTEs of ego-driven and power-hungry people. His CTE created an environment of anxiety and fear of failure, and in this way, he got his results quickly. Well done him, again! After he was finished, the schools would need to spend three years recovering from the trauma. All the resources had usually been spent on the current year groups taking examinations (leaving the next year's groups to take the exams underfunded and undereducated and therefore much more likely to fail). The damage that his CTE did to the staff was, for some, irreversible and resulted in talented teachers losing their passion and leaving the profession for good. But, never mind. It couldn't be his fault as he had won an award. It did not matter to him that, as with Moira, there was absolutely no joy in any of the schools he 'saved'. There was no pleasure or inspiration in any aspect of the students' learning. None whatsoever. They were taught to pass exams, not to learn or to evolve as people. But what a good job he did! So much better than anyone else. Well done him, again and again!

There was another head teacher, Samantha, who wanted her school to encourage independent learning. Young but wise beyond her years, she realised that her staff would have to be independent learners too if this was to happen. She studied leadership techniques and learnt what to do to empower them. However, she was unaware that her understanding of 'empowering her staff' was really only tokenistic and demonstrated. The expectation from Samantha was therefore that staff only needed to demonstrate independent learning and empowerment because she believed this to be the 'real thing'. They were not expected to experience it and live it fully. They were not inspired by her to go beyond this artificial tick-box version because they were not encouraged to accept its existence. The students, in turn, mistakenly learnt from the CTE of the staff that demonstration of independent learning was all that was required. The head's leadership technique was inspected many times, and each time she passed with such flying colours that she was put on a pedestal and lauded as a role model for other heads. Gradually, because of her 'success', those in education increasingly believed that empowerment of staff meant only tokenistic empowerment. They also learnt that independent learning meant only tokenistic independent learning. Sadly, this technique became the norm as more and more schools were persuaded to adopt her model.

There was another head teacher: an ambitious young man called Jack. His technique was a little rough around the edges to begin with, but he had a clear ambition for his environment. He wanted it to be full of strong and independent people at all levels. He felt that this would create the perfect environment for his students to thrive. His CTE was perfectly aligned with the task. Nothing was a demonstration or a pretence. At first, his senior leaders were confused. They had got used to being told what to do by the old head, and all their work was usually overseen. So, when their opinions were asked for, and independence expected, they would say amongst themselves that they felt 'unsupported'. However, slowly but surely, they began to embrace their power and the level of accountability it entailed. They began to thrive. The group found themselves genuinely motivated at work and excited to go into school each day despite the pressures of the role. Their newfound strength was reflected in their CTEs, and so the ethos permeated through to the rest of the members of staff. Although there were one or two cynical teachers who did not really respond to the changes, the vast majority in the school were lifted. After a year, the school moved from being a 'failing' school to one that was described as 'good'. This particular head had an eye on the long-term sustainability of what he was doing, and because his CTE was genuinely of this nature, progress was consistent and enabled the staff to build strong foundations for growth. Staff continued to be challenged but were very content – gradually becoming nourished by the organisation that was expecting so much of them. They were able to offer more of themselves. Eventually, the head moved on to a different school and the next head to be employed witnessed the school becoming 'outstanding'. The old head was delighted that he had set up such a structure for long-term change. He won no awards and never would, but the school went on to thrive afterwards and there was often laughter in its corridors.

All these four heads were under the same sort of pressures and each dealt with them differently. The first two bowed to the pressure of narrow expectation, and so the pressure's dark and reactive nature infiltrated their CTE. They became at one with it – it became who they were. The third head, under the same pressure of expectation, sought out a different answer but only found it superficially. Even though she thought her actions to be effective, they never moved beyond artifice. The fourth head filtered and disarmed the pressure he was experiencing without going into battle with it. He achieved this feat simply by *working on*, *becoming,* and eventually *being* an excellent leader. His CTE was therefore steady, consistent, powerful and patient. His genuine persona meant he was able to forge a pathway forwards, disabling the initial pressures everyone else in the environment was feeling. Like the best leaders, he did not feel stress and tension despite his environment, and this was reflected in his CTE. His team were then inspired by him to eventually become the independent and individual stars of the show. Better still, they became people who, via their improved CTEs, inspired others to become the same: a domino effect. It is fair to say that this particular head understood the nature of the CTE well. Even though the third and fourth heads may have been using similar techniques, the outcomes were different because they were different people. One was an authentic leader, the other was pretending.

When you have achieved a healthy and genuine CTE, you will be able to impact everyone around you in a positive and sustainable way. But your healthy CTE may take time to permeate your organisation. If those around you have been used to experiencing a destructive CTE from others in charge, they will have developed a defensiveness to cope with the situation. Initially, their CTEs might cause a type of blocking effect to yours because they do not recognise your level of authenticity.

Take a moment to consider this next story.

Zara, Doug & the Boat on the Thames

Zara and Doug run a speedboat trip on the Thames. They take about twenty passengers at a time for fifty minutes or so. Their reviews are almost exclusively five star, and everyone says that it is the most exciting and invigorating thing they have done in London. Well, almost everybody. Very occasionally there will be a single 'know it all', or perhaps a couple, who tell Zara and Dug how to run their trip and loudly voice their opinions and 'expertise' from the sidelines. How they manage to keep talking while going that fast on the river is a mystery. Zara noticed that this type of person tends to affect the feel of the boat for the others on it, and so she turned to a coach to ask for advice. The coach said the following, 'You have an obligation to placate the person drawing attention to themselves because it is your responsibility to maintain the enjoyment of the boat for everyone.' The coach then proceeded to give Zara techniques designed to quieten people such as these who are negative without needing to confront them. Then he said, 'You have an obvious love of your job and the river. If you allow this joy to be present with the know-it-alls then two things will happen. First, you will not negatively impact the rest of the boat as you use your techniques to deal with these people because your love of the river will continuously permeate the atmosphere, no matter what you are doing. You will be allowing your love for the river to be stronger and more authentic than their need for attention. Your positivity will then naturally take charge of the environment. The rest of the boat will love the experience of the trip because you love it. You love it so much more than the arrogant person needs to be heard. Second, you will not have empowered the pompous person because you will not have been limited by them. There may even be a third thing that happens. In this environment, the know-it-all may actually stop their monologue and begin to relax into the trip. In this scenario, you have infected the other person with your own positive attitude. Sometimes miracles do happen!'

There may be people that you feel cannot be affected by your CTE. These people are likely to have been so exposed to the negative impact of the darker side of the human condition, and therefore the darker nature of the Complete Transmission Experience, that they may have shut down and be closed to any feelings at all. They have developed an impenetrable CTE defence barrier. But, as you can see from the story of Olive, below, they can still be helped.

Olive the Sports Coach

There was a coach called Olive who worked with a small group of elite figure skaters. One of these was Jackson. Jackson, when young, was a superbly natural skater and as brave as a lion. Then something happened to Jackson and he needed to be moved from one home to another, quickly. After that, whenever he was given advice by Olive to help him improve, he would not progress as he had previously done. Jackson's indescribable ability was lost and, much as he tried, he could not seem to move beyond a double axel with his jumps. Occasionally, more by luck than judgement, he would manage a triple loop, but it was never something he could rely on. To make matters worse, Jackson's body would seem to turn against him before every competition and he would almost always find himself injured and unable to take part. As time passed, the other skaters of his age in the group either progressed beyond Jackson's ability (and were regularly landing quads) or left altogether to pursue other interests, bored with the hard work and the pain of falling. As you might expect, on many occasions, Olive was advised by the skating federation that Jackson should no longer be part of the group. He was now too far behind to compete at the Nationals. But Olive never once considered removing him. She knew that, for Jackson, the skating environment was the one thing that kept him afloat, and sane. To Olive, these reasons were more precious than any jump he could ever land. Had he hindered the group then Olive's decision might have been different – but he did not. Younger members were sometimes joining and so Jackson never seemed to stand out as the least skilled. Olive knew that the value of skating was different for everyone. Incidentally, Olive was one of a handful of coaches in the world who could inspire the elite to greatness in this difficult sport and still remain aware of her responsibility to all of her athletes.

In the story, the coach comes up against what first seems to be an impenetrable CTE defence barrier in the form of her trauma-ridden athlete. While he cannot be reached when it comes to improving his athletic skills, he can absolutely be helped via the strong empathic nature of his coach's CTE and the environment she creates. It could also be argued that the rest of the group, experiencing the same environment that permeates their training, might also be better for it.

Another group of people who can seem 'closed' to your CTE but who can be helped by you in similar ways to Jackson are those who have developed deeply complex and well-practised defence systems. An example might be someone who has spent their life being a martyr to the cause. They see this way of being as the single focus of their existence and do not for one moment consider that their steady judgement of you and of others (while presenting a front of being complimentary or approving) is in any way a problem. But, if your CTE is balanced and healthy, you might find that even if they are emotionally 'closed' to you they will still turn up to meet you, week after week, despite making little or no progress towards their supposed goals. They are drawn to you because your CTE is healthy and a hidden part of them feels good to be there.

Less extreme examples in coaching might be a client who, every time you meet, will tell you that they have had no issues during the week whatsoever. None. They will wait for you to drive the session and only speak when they want to finish your sentences for you. But, still they turn up on time, week after week. Traditionally it might be argued that it is the coach's job to help this type of client achieve some goal or another, but if the client is unreachable (rather than just difficult, as perhaps one in a hundred might be), then you still have something to give them that can be of benefit – a place to be for a while. Just because an irreversible switch seems to have been flicked on inside them, does not mean that they can't be helped by sitting with you. The environment your healthy CTE creates is as important to these people as it is to those looking to achieve their specific aspirations. It is just that the conversation is different. Perhaps your sessions are the only sense of healthy belonging they are able to accept.

Your responsibility as a teacher, coach or counsellor is therefore substantial, even when you're not traditionally teaching, coaching or counselling. Depending on your CTE, you can either create a positive environment which gives the student or client a healthy place to grow, a superficial environment that encourages them to be artificial whenever they are with you, or, in the worst of cases, a dark environment that cannot help but systematically bring them down. If you imagine how many students or clients you might encounter in a lifetime, you will begin to get an idea of the impact your CTE might be having. If you are intrinsically valuing the individual without artifice, then they, in turn, are likely to feel individually valued. This will come about because they are actually being individually valued, without pretence, rather than valued in an artificial way.

And what happens if we take this understanding of our CTE to its natural conclusion within the wider community? With a healthy CTE it becomes possible for you to encourage sustainable growth and wellbeing, continuously and entirely free of charge, amongst everyone who comes in contact with you. If your CTE is uplifting, you will affect the people you meet. Then those you meet, having been lifted by you will, via their own raised CTEs, inspire others to go on to be lifted and so on. There will be easy and healthy sustainable community growth that is natural and nourishing. That is the Complete Transmission Experience and its potential is limitless. What could be a more perfect system?

The bright feel of the room encourages in you a sense of natural ease. It's a good time to release any further tension you might be holding.

Tension-Releasing Exercises: Level Three

In the previous rooms we have become aware of the emotional effects of tension by sensing our reaction to others who are tense. We then increased this awareness by looking at the trigger points that stimulate our own tension. Now, in this room, we will be exploring our tension still further by becoming aware of its nature moment to moment. In doing so, we will be able to release it without going into battle with it.

Inside and Out

- *Sit in a café, close to a window, and notice the tension in those around you. Do not seek to judge them or alter them, simply notice how they make you feel. Each time you experience someone who is tense allow this experience to deepen a tension free feeling within yourself.*

- *Now move your attention through the window to those outside of the café in the street. Notice their tension and how it makes you feel. It is very likely that most of those you observe will be tense (in the form of some kind of stress) because they are in a relatively unpredictable situation. Again, allow your feeling of being tension free to grow from the safety of where you are sitting. Every time you see someone showing the least sign of tension, release more tension in yourself. Do not worry if you feel you are already tension free. You will discover that there are infinite layers to this exercise.*

- *Eventually, when you are ready, walk out of the café into the stream of tense passers-by. As you remain supremely tension free, begin to notice the sense of natural empowerment that comes about when you are so free of tension in a tense environment that everything feels effortless.*

- *Remember we are developing the type of tension free way of being that makes us more aware of our surroundings not less. If you feel in any way dazed or sleepy during this exercise do not go outside until you are fully recovered. We need to be alert in a busy street.*

- *Repeat the exercise.*

Maintaining the Groove

- *Imagine a silky smooth and tension free groove that runs ever so slightly downhill, just enough to develop a gentle natural momentum. When you wake up in the morning and you are feeling at your most tension free, imagine yourself to be a ball rolling in this groove.*

- *Keep the ball rolling throughout your working day. If a bump in your day occurs and you find yourself out of the groove, as you undoubtably will, there is nothing to worry about. Simply dust yourself off and, when you are ready, return to your tension free groove and continue.*

Once you get a feel for what it is like to be tension free, regardless of your surroundings or the events of your day, you will no longer be the victim of your environment and your CTE will show that. Everything will feel different. Many of the most successful people in education, coaching and counselling are able to work without tension using these techniques, so why shouldn't you?

The Inner Chambers

Consider the story *Code Breaker* before entering.

Code Breaker

Imagine you are taking part in a game called 'code breaker'. Your leader introduces the game with a verbal code. She says, 'I am wearing brown shoes' (when her shoes are actually black). You then have to try to mimic the code in order to win the game. You say, 'my jumper is pink' (when it is really grey) or 'my trousers are blue' (when they are black). But each time you are wrong. What is going on? You can't seem to break the code even though you think you are observing the rules. After a while, another member of your group stumbles across the key. It is not the phrase that is spoken that represents the code at all; it is the fact that the leader scratches her nose as she says it. The spoken phrase is designed to point your attention towards something of less importance – the words. It is a diversion. Of course, once the person has the key, it is easy for her to break the code time and time again. Eventually, you pick up on the trick too, much to the chagrin of those in your group who are known to be 'cleverer' than you but cannot for the life of them figure it out.

The rooms that follow are a more secretive affair.

Room Seven

You wander through an entrance hall into a bright room.

There are four vermilion pillars framing a mountain view.

The floor is scattered with turquoise cushions.

You have finally reached the room in which we can begin to explore the question you have been asking: 'How can I significantly raise my CTE?'

To explore the method of raising our CTE, we first need to understand something of the subject of *acquired learning*.

You sit.

Acquired Learning

Acquired learning is a Taoist notion that appears partly open and partly obscured within the Taoist text the Tao Te Ching. It holds within it a practical key to understanding how to lift and nourish your CTE. There are likely to be many other ways of lifting your CTE but, in the Nine Rooms, acquired learning has been selected for three reasons. First, my first personal experience of the dimension was in a Taoist context, and so it makes sense to explain it using Taoist principles. Second, the removal of acquired learning, as captured in Taoist writings, is closely related to removing artificiality from our lives and therefore resonates with our understanding of improving the authenticity of our CTE. Third, Taoism as a practical way of seeing the world is inclusive. It welcomes everyone regardless of spiritual belief (or no spiritual belief). In fact, when it comes to Taoism, the gateways of understanding are only limited to our understanding of ourselves. It is a type of failsafe device that limits the misuse of power. For example, if an explanation uses storytelling or metaphor (as it often does), the depth to which the reader resonates with the message is directly related to how well they understand themselves in relation to their life experience. An old man concerned only with his frequent visits to the hospital for minor ailments will not interpret a metaphor in the same way as an enlightened old man, wandering the mountains.

The Tao Te Ching contains a phrase you might already know: (roughly translated) 'The journey of a thousand miles begins with a single step', which has inspired a great many to start their journeys and might also be quite apt for your journey here.

In order to secure and disseminate its teachings, Taoism favours the oral tradition which, despite what you might expect, is very reliable when it comes to consistency. A common misconception is that information is passed down *only* via word of mouth. If this was the case, it would be open to reinterpretation across the generations and the original meanings would most certainly be altered, even obscured to the point of being lost. The details of how the oral tradition works are not relevant here, but suffice it to say that it is related to a secret, sophisticated and targeted understanding of the process of transmission.

It's important, therefore, to find someone to whom the 'oral' interpretation has been authentically passed. For our interpretation of acquired learning I have drawn on the experience of two Taoist masters who live and breathe the Tao Te Ching, have authentic experience of Taoist transmission, and know of its benefits well. I have met with them, sat with them, talked with them and interviewed them. I have also gained their trust. We have formed an agreement that I may reveal some of the nature of acquired learning here, on the understanding that it is dealt with respectfully.

It is fair to say that what is revealed in this room only scrapes the surface of the knowledge of the Taoist notion of acquired learning. It certainly does not approach the more secretive inner understandings, but this is more than enough to guide us authentically on our way.

The Meaning of Acquired Learning

Your acquired learning is all the learning that has been impressed upon you that you may have come to believe serves you well but in fact does not. From its place, hidden in plain sight, your acquired learning subtly inhibits all that you do – all that you are. In fact, your acquired learning permeates your being so entirely that it creates what a Taoist would call a 'false heart'. (The heart in Taoist practice represents the place from which all our emotions and decisions derive.) It is extremely likely that all of us are acting from a 'false heart' to varying degrees. The situation comes about mainly due to the social conditioning we have experienced, and continue to experience, from a very young age.

With the generation of a 'false heart' comes something called *acquired action*. Acquired action is the action taken by us that derives from our acquired learning. Acquired action then leads to the necessity for more acquired learning to support it, to justify it, and so the cycle deepens. It repeats and repeats to become our ingrained reality. This circular pattern is something I have called the *acquired cycle*.

Acquired action can show itself in a number of different guises: self-righteousness, taking yourself too seriously, lack of spontaneous humour and laughter, pomposity, pretentiousness, the need to put on a front, keeping up with the Joneses or what Freud has called, 'the vanity of small differences'. The acquired cycle is also frequently found in organisations where the foundations are inauthentic: schools with core aims that sit nicely in a frame on the wall and are only actioned in a tokenistic way are a common example.

If we look to the effect our acquired learning can have on our clients, students and children, the impact can be quite startling. Our acquired learning creates our 'false heart'. Our 'false heart' brings about our acquired action. Therefore, because who we are and how we are being is transmitted via our CTE, our CTE transmits our 'false heart' to our clients and students moment to moment, day after day, year after year. They are negatively impacted by our 'false heart' and our engagement in our acquired cycle.

The opposite of the 'false heart' is the 'true heart'. The 'true heart' is achieved when our acquired learning no longer impacts our lives. The acquired cycle is replaced with the non-acquired cycle – and with it comes a sense of clarity and understanding that cannot be achieved if our heart is 'false'. Of course, unless you are a guru or a Taoist master, or have the time to sit on a mountain for decades, this state is unlikely to be fully achieved by us. However, what can be achieved is a gradual change from the 'false heart' towards the 'true heart'. We can be on the journey. We can gradually move from a sense of the contrived that derives from the 'false heart', to a fundamental state of authenticity that only comes from the development of the 'true heart'. This movement is then reflected in the quality of our CTE and so lifts those in our vicinity. For us as coaches, teachers, leaders, therapists, counsellors and parents it can be seen as a type of personal unveiling, to discover the healthier person underneath.

Replacing the 'False Heart' with the 'True Heart'

To understand how the 'false heart' can move towards the 'true heart' consider the metaphor of a cup of dirty water. You might think that the best thing to do would be to tip the water out of the cup (representing quickly removing the influence our acquired learning has on us) and to replace it with clean, fresh water (so we can continue our journey suddenly fully refreshed, with a 'true heart'). But this is not the case. The process for us needs to be more gradual if it is to work in the reality of our environment.

Metaphorically speaking, we do the following:

- We take our cup of dirty water and place a second empty cup next to it.
- In our second cup we pour a little of the dirty water from the first – a couple of drops.
- We filter the few drops of water until it is clean.
- We then pour the clean water back into the dirty water.
- We repeat.
- Slowly but surely the dirty water becomes clearer and clearer as we begin to reverse the acquired cycle. Every drop cleaned represents us clearing out some of our acquired learning as we edge closer and closer towards a 'true heart'. In other words, the 'false heart' gradually becomes less and less 'false' and, gradually, an increasing sense of being well emerges. This improvement is reflected in our CTE and so is passed on to others.

Removing Your Acquired Learning in Practice

To recognise and remove your acquired learning, you can follow the steps outlined here. Should you want a detailed program there is a book that accompanies *Nine Rooms*, entitled *Nine Rooms Workbook – 81 days*. It is a practical, 81-day guide designed to gradually alleviate the hold your acquired learning has over you. For now, here are some ideas that will serve you very effectively.

Exercise One – Focusing on Awareness

First and foremost, know that you are seeking to remove your acquired learning by focusing on the effect your acquired learning is having on you – the power it holds over your decision making and over how you are being. Once recognised, the negative influence of your acquired learning (and therefore the acquired cycle) will begin to wane. Similarly, you are looking to bring to light the negative feelings that accompany these acquired actions. These feelings, untranslated, felt in the moment, are what will slowly educate your heart. They will gradually transform it from false to true, simply by being felt.

- *Ponder the above.*

Exercise Two – The Method of Removing Acquired Learning

The methodology is very straightforward. It contains no drama or emotional struggle whatsoever.

- *Lead yourself into the process by exploring the acquired cycles of your organisation. Identify any action whatsoever at work that you already know does not properly serve the cause. For example, as a teacher you might realise that your students' reports are far from being truthfully written to the point of being misleading for the parents. As a counsellor you may have to report on your progress and are finding this action counterproductive when it comes to the genuine progression of your clients. In many organisations it may also be true that the importance of the paperwork that supports a task supersedes the importance of the task itself. Notice the feel of these revelations, but do not seek to change them.*

- *Now take a look at the impact this acquired action is having on your students and clients. Notice how this feels to you.*

- *Now think to the acquired cycles that have brought this situation into being. For the teacher, it might be a government, determined to prove itself in an educational context, that can understand no other way of improving standards than to persuade schools to stretch the truth. Or, for the coach, it may be that there is a university-affiliated counselling system that insists on a certain way of working to demonstrate legitimacy and to secure funds. Don't cast judgement – just notice and ponder.*

- *Allow yourself to begin to recognise how many of these systems are accepted as 'just the way things are'. Ponder on how deeply they go and how they feel. Once realised, consider this question. 'Does one cycle reveal another that has become more deeply embedded?' Remember, no judgement.*

- *Look to your students and clients again. How has it got to the stage that you find yourself persuading them to partake in the acquired cycles of the organisation? Do not judge, just notice and ponder.*

- *Look around your environment at the acquired cycles of others. How does their 'false heart' make them react to life? How does being with them feel to you in the moment? Again, notice and ponder.*

- *Now, begin to question how many of these same patterns and systems you have bought into. How responsible are you for perpetuating these established patterns? Generally, how does your 'false heart' make you react to life at work? Do not judge, just notice and ponder.*

Consider these examples from a teacher's perspective:

- *If you think you are spending too much time report writing, how often have you found yourself putting pressure on the teachers in your charge to make their reports more detailed even though you do not believe in its value?*
- *If you are a parent, how often have you scrutinised your own child's report and used it as a basis for criticism when you know it is, at best, a shallow reflection of their learning?*
- *How often have you praised your own children for an improved report when you know, in your heart, it means less than the praise you are giving?*
- *How often have you used reporting as a control mechanism? How much has this become the norm?*
- *What areas of teaching and learning have you bought into just because this is the way things are and it's easier not to question them?*

- *How often have you used guilt to try to persuade your students to improve their behaviour in class and praised them when they have done better?*

- *If you are a parent who has said you want your child to be happy, how often has this idea disintegrated at the first sign of any problem whatsoever from the school?*

- *How often have you thought a student to be 'good' if they knuckled down and 'bad' if they have not?*

What about acquired cycles in your personal life? What do they bring about? Ponder these questions below.

- *What acquired cycles have you been taught to respect in your personal life? How many do you buy into in the name of keeping social order? How many do you perpetuate? How much of your acquired learning has been integrated into your understanding of 'respect'?*

You stand and move to the view. You take a moment to reflect:

How honest are you being with yourself? Is it worth starting the exercise again and looking more truthfully this time? Remember, acquired cycles are everywhere.

Important is not to change your actions because of what you find. The work is about bringing your acquired learning to the light and seeing how you feel, not forcing external change. We are merely looking to alleviate the power our acquired learning holds over us by allowing our emotions to surface and to educate us. In doing so, we raise our CTE.

To start this journey is to truly open your own Pandora's box as more and more is revealed that leads to an ocean of something else deeper but fathomable. However, unlike poor Pandora, when these things are brought into the light, their power to restrict you greatly reduces. As we have said, they hold much more power hidden than set free – so set them free.

Exercise Three – The Power of Nonaction or 'Shining the Light'

The Taoist way is sometimes described as nonaction or even inaction. Consider the value of the following.

- Remember, our only call to action is to shine a light, both internally (how we feel about our acquired learning) and externally (how we feel about the effect acquired learning is having on others). In doing so, we bring it out of the dark. Imagine yourself growing simply because of your realisations about acquired learning.

- ❖ Consider the amount of energy it would take to try to change acquired cycles from the outside in – the number of unnecessary battles you would be drawn into time and time again. If I was a teacher and I refused to write my reports, I would lose my job. If I was a coach and refused to partake in a practice that my governing body deemed essential, then I would be suspended.

- ❖ This is one reason we do not seek to change the outward appearance of acquired learning. It is knowing it is acquired that is the key to being released from it, and this will inevitably affect change in others via our CTE.

- ❖ In order to affect change, we (our CTEs) need to be at the centre of things. We are no good to anyone if we are at home twiddling our thumbs from the sidelines instead of interacting with our students or clients. When it comes to our CTE, we need to be there to create the change.

As we have said, shining the light is all that is necessary. Illumination leads to indescribable personal growth, and this growth cannot *not* be reflected in your CTE. To do anything more than shine a light would be counterproductive. For example, should you become angry at what you realise (a form of judgement) then this will be reflected in your CTE and reverse your progress. But this type of angry reaction is natural, so how do you deal with it when it occurs?

Consider these five steps below:

1. *Recognise the feeling of anger (or any emotional response) as a sign that what you have realised about yourself or others is important to you. Be grateful that it has jumped to your attention.*

2. *See the emotion that has arisen as a call to action rather than as something negative.*

3. *Do not, under any circumstances, take external action because of the emotion. Instead, just let the feeling be there. Now, let the label of your feeling go. You will realise that, once it is unnamed, you are left with a type of energy rather than a named emotional response.*

4 *At this point you have a choice. You can let the emotional energy become circular, living with it for years and years as a more and more practised response to this issue (supporting the 'false heart'), or you can focus the energy towards nourishing your CTE (developing the 'true heart').*

5 *You can move the energy to your advantage by i) remaining tension free as you feel the feeling. This allows it to transform from one intention to another, ii) recognising that the feeling is the exact experience you are encouraging in yourself to educate your false heart, iii) knowing that when the feeling is unnamed it is much easier to let the energy go, iv) allowing the energy to rise and fall in its own time.*

In this way, nothing externally will be challenged but your CTE will be improving day by day. There will be no battles with others, no conflicts and no confrontations. You will only be focusing on your own personal growth.

Signs

As you make progress using the exercises, there are various signs that will appear to let you know you are on the right track:

- People will approach you slightly differently to before, so be ready for a bit more fluidity and openness from them.
- Things will begin to feel lighter and easier, and you will find yourself pulled less and less into destructive situations.
- There will be more lightness and laughter around you.
- The acquired cycle takes a great deal of contrived effort to maintain – the unacquired far less so. Expect to be more energised.
- You will not be unnecessarily emotionally influenced by the false hearts of others anymore.
- You will begin to forget how you used to be and will find it difficult to make comparisons to how you were in the past. (However, you will find people making them for you: 'You look well today.')
- You will find yourself sailing through your acquired tasks with ease because they no longer have an emotional hold on you. By doing this, you will inspire others to be the same way. You will find yourself far less judgemental and far more proactive.

If you do not see these signs begin to appear almost immediately then you may wish to consider the following.

A mistake novices tend to make is to become overly aware of the fact they are exploring the removal of their acquired learning. They might think that the process is somehow 'special' and 'important'. For example, if I became hugely aware of a piece of acquired action I was taking, then I might walk into a room the next day expecting people to act differently towards me because of what I have discovered about myself the day before – and they don't. This lack of reaction from others comes about precisely because my CTE contains my awareness that I am somehow doing something 'special' or 'important' and this supersedes my learning. As the Taoists might say, always work with humility, simplicity and humour.

You just need to focus on feeling as much of your acquired learning as you can. The exercise ends there. Let the signs come to you and surprise you rather than going looking for them. Remember, a brightly coloured flower does not go looking for a bee. The bee is attracted to how the flower is – what it has become once it's bloomed.

To summarise, we are seeking to clarify our acquired cycle by putting ourselves on the journey from the 'false heart' to the 'true heart'. In doing so, our CTE improves slowly but surely because we improve with the emotional release of what has been holding us back.

Remember: no judgement, only realisation.

Onwards and upwards.

Please read *Lost in Translation* as you travel to the next room.

Lost in Translation

The master sat with his teenage ward who had been busy on the internet and was full of a single question. 'The zero-point field, in physics,' she said, 'contains all of the information of the universe – everything past, present and future.' She took a breath. 'I have read that the zero-point field contains the quantum foam which has energy called zero-point energy. Nothingness has energy that can be measured!' she exclaimed. 'What's your question?' asked the master, encouraging his ward to get to the point. 'It's not my question,' she responded. 'It's someone else's.' 'Never a good start,' said the master. The ward hesitated, confused. 'Well,' she continued, 'they say that if we can translate the information of the zero-point field into language, especially the language of physics and mathematics, we will know everything there is to know. So, their question is, my question is, how do they go about translating it?'

The master did not need to think. 'You cannot find the answer you seek from that question,' he said, 'because that's the wrong question.' The ward did not understand

and so felt it her duty to ask, 'So, what is the right question?' The master smiled. 'You will always know the right question because it always has an obvious answer.'

'So,' repeated the ward now a little frustrated, 'what is the right question?' 'There are two right questions,' replied the master. The ward sighed. 'First, why does the zero-point field need to be translated at all? Why put it into words when its original language is to be sensed and felt? You feel it all the time when you meditate. You know the energy is there and you are beginning to learn how to use it, so why is translation into words necessary? Second, rather than translate it, why not learn to converse with it in its original tongue – the felt sense? It is truly the universal language, so why not communicate with it in a way it understands; in a way we all understand? The only form of perfect translation is for you to feel it in its original state and to see what this feeling translates to – in yourself. What does it inspire you to do better or differently? What new ideas does it bring about?' The ward listened intently but she still seemed confused and remained silent, so the master continued. 'Your answer is simply to meditate and to be with the source. Feel its immense knowledge, its fathomless value, and then act on those feelings. This is how to communicate and learn from it.'

The ward did not understand a word the master had said, but she thanked him for his conversation. She sat with him for a while, took some tea, and then went on her way, happier than when she arrived.

Room Eight

You have reached the penultimate room.

It's freshly painted green, but there's nothing in it except a ladder and a few dust sheets.

You can hear voices outside, laughing and joking.

Here you will explore the nature
of attunement and its magical potential
to lift your CTE to extraordinary levels.

Consider the story of Samuel.

Samuel's Music

You may be surprised to learn that some Taoist masters have children. One such child was Samuel, or Samu for short. From a young age, Samu loved to listen to all kinds of music but he was particularly attracted to the sound of a type of flute called the xiao. Whenever he could find a xiao player (usually sitting around a corner, behind a tree, or somewhere else that might surprise a passer-by with wonderful music when they least expected to hear it), Samu would listen away for hours. When he got his own xiao at the age of five, Samu would play whenever and wherever he could, sometimes accidentally finding his way towards tunes. On occasion, he would escape the house to surprise passers-by. He would jump out in front of them from behind bushes or play to a dog whose owner was not pleased to be held up. (Samu did not yet understand the difference between shocking people and uplifting them when it came to the unexpected.) When he was eight, Samu's mother introduced him to a teacher of music called Mr Chang who himself was a virtuoso on the xiao but who also played the dizi (a similar flute to the xiao but with softer and more rustic tones). By the time Samu was fifteen he had switched to the dizi. From the first time he played the instrument, he sensed a type of conversation was happening in the music between the spirits and himself, and he enjoyed the interaction very much. At twenty, Samu no longer had to think about technique, notes or rhythms or where to place himself when he played outside for the element of surprise. He would just go out and converse with the spirits through his dizi and passers-by, surprised to find such wonderful music on a mountain, in a town or outside a school, would stop and listen for hours as Samu did when he was a child. Then, on his thirtieth birthday, Samu was invited to purchase a very old dizi that had been carefully hidden away in the back of an old music shop, for decades. It was an instrument only allowed to be bought and played by those thought to be masters.

How Does Attunement Work?

Attunement begins with alignment. Alignment, in this instance, is you knowing the technical side of your craft so well that you no longer have to think about it as you work. You understand the left-hand side of the equation so completely that you no longer have to focus on it at all. Think of a teacher in the flow of a lesson who is simply connected with the class and enjoying the fluidity of the experience; a therapist not thinking about technique and knowing she will say the right thing as she speaks to her client. It is the type of expertise that opens the door to the possibility of the right-hand side of the equation taking control. By merging with your technique in this way, the potential for something extraordinary happens: attunement.

Attunement is a way of being that creates an elevated connection space. Via your CTE, you connect with your class, your client or your team. An obvious example of attunement might be theatre actors performing in a great play. They are so aligned with their craft that they become attuned, and in doing so, they lift and inspire the audience, seemingly with ease. They take them to an elevated space where audience and actor communicate in a way that's altogether different to how we communicate in everyday life. It is how these actors are being which leads them to perform as they do and to have the effect that they do. In these circumstances, it is not unusual for those in the audience in physical and emotional pain to forget their disease when they are at the theatre. Another example might be a concert violinist who is so at one with her technique and the music that the audience feels transported into another plain of being and somehow joins her there. Such an occurrence is not uncommon. It might even be something we have grown to expect from our classical musicians and our acting greats.

In teaching, coaching and counselling situations, if we can appreciate our work as a creative form, we can find a comparable potential to lift and inspire our students and clients. We too can align with our craft and become attuned. We have the opportunity to see our work as an improvisation, a piece of jazz or unrehearsed acting, where instinct and timing come to the fore and blend with impeccable technique to open the door to this other level of being.

In fact, teaching can be likened to acting in this way: if the teacher hides behind a mask, and behind her technique, and has to refer to a lesson plan to know what to say, this can be compared to bad acting, and so attunement cannot occur to lift the class. However, should the opposite happen, and the teacher and the technique appear as one effortless singularity, not only can the teacher's attunement invite the class to a lifted space, the event can happen more and more easily as the class begin to know how the teacher 'is', and to expect this way of being every lesson. This lift can go so far as to be anticipated before each session. As with expectant crowds waiting to see a well-loved actor, the anticipation means that the communicative job of the teacher is already half done. The audience may stand and clap the moment the actor walks on stage, before they have even said a single word – already they are elevated to a shared lifted state. Similarly, the teacher will have the class in the palm of her hand before she even walks into the classroom.

On the other hand, when unaligned there can be no sustainable attunement. An unaligned performance of a play may be intellectually appreciated by the audience (left-hand side), but the experience will not lift them to an improved place (right-hand side). The same applies to the concert violinist whose tuning and technique is not up to scratch. The moment the first couple of out of tune notes are played, the prospect of alignment and therefore attunement and the lifted plain evaporate. In a play or a concert, it only takes one person in the group to be unaligned to ruin the possibility of lift for the entire piece.

Alignment and Tension

Alignment is not necessarily linked to calmness and serenity, but it is directly linked to a lack of tension. Remember we are aiming for the type of 'tension freeness' that enables an athlete to run faster, not for us to become blasé about our role. We require a lack of tension to align because our technique needs to be able to fall effortlessly into place and tension will inhibit this process. In some sporting situations, the relationship between coach and athlete can be fiery, but this doesn't necessarily mean the coach can't become aligned. There is a distinct difference between being feisty and challenging while being open and tension free (a situation that *can* lead to alignment), and being moody, angry and tension-filled as you challenge your athlete (a situation that *cannot* lead to alignment). A love-hate relationship can be good or bad, it all depends on the level of tension held and caused.

In some instances, where there is absolutely no negative tension and an immense amount of goodwill, it's just about possible for someone to attune for a short while even if they are not aligned with superior technique. If a child play-acts a situation with absolute involvement, they are forgiven their technical mistakes because of the connection they create with any onlookers. Their attunement occurs because of their total engagement with their performance, not because of their skill. It is fair to say that under these circumstances most of the audience may well become distracted after an initial period of being enthralled. The brashness and the out of tune singing of the performer can begin to become an issue, and so the attunement doesn't last for long. The same can be said of young teachers who are adored by their classes because of their personalities and their naturally energetic nature. Their classes can become instantly attuned despite the teacher's lack of experience, technique and knowledge. However, if the teacher cannot hold class discipline or if they lack significant subject knowledge, they may only be forgiven for a short period of time before disorder and the failing of exams become an 'issue' and attunement is lost.

Finally, as our ability to attune improves, so do we, and therefore so does our CTE. Every time a concert pianist performs attuned, their understanding of the indescribable nature of attunement is consolidated. They begin to get a feel for the state and the sense of play it brings about in them, and they grow holistically as performers. The same can be true for coaches, teachers, leaders, therapists and counsellors. Once we find the feel of the attuned space, our craft becomes so much more effective and so much easier and more pleasurable for us to access. Time disappears.

Attunement might be said to encourage a sense of well-earned freedom. The hard, technical work has been done and we are now freer to enjoy what we do. It's addictive too. The more you have, the more you want. What could be a better reason for coming to work or for your clients or students to come to school, coaching or their therapy sessions?

Moving from Aligned to Attuned

To move yourself from being aligned (where you are already tension free) to attuned requires one more thing – a lack of self-consciousness. Many football players on the pitch cannot attune as they are too self-conscious when they play in front of large crowds. They only demonstrate their abilities during the match as a bad actor might when play-acting to the crowd. The difference between them and the really great players is that the greats always play freely and in an uninhibited fashion even in the most pressured of situations. The real greats are the few people who might be able to encourage the crowd to attune despite a poor performance from the rest of the team. Their alignment with their craft is such that it supersedes everyone else's lack of alignment on the pitch.

Becoming Attuned

It may take a while, but these are the principles that will help you achieve attunement:

- *Work on the release of physical and mental tension in order to first become truly aligned to your craft. It will provide a strong base for your attunement. (You can use the exercises in these chambers or those in the Nine Rooms Workbook to achieve this state.)*

- *Know your subject and the technique of your craft like the back of your hand. Make sure you make time for technical practice and improvement every day. Keep developing in this area. Know that it is never ending.*

- *If you are a teacher, identify another teacher who aligns with their craft. Their lessons are likely to be light, fun and have a natural momentum about them. There will be little that is artificial or forced. It may be best described as a 'buzzy' environment. Most importantly, the teacher will be genuinely enjoying what they are doing.*

- *Go into that environment and help out. Do not analyse anything – just get a feel for the atmosphere and how that teacher is 'being'. Do not copy. Just tune in. Repeat, repeat and repeat.*

- *Then, rather than mimicking the other teacher's attuned style, in your own way, 'be' attuned with your own classes. It is the feel you are recreating, nothing else. It may take a little while, but you will get there. You may wish to start with your 'easier' classes and work your way to those more challenging.*

- *There are likely to be occasions in your social life when you are naturally attuned. One example might be going out with your friends where you are no longer self-conscious and do not hold any tension. Time seems to go in a flash. Know that, although this example is a million miles away from your responsible role at work, the energetic space, the attunement that you and your friends might feel, is remarkably similar to the one you are trying to create in your professional context.*

- *If you know anyone aligned, in a healthy way, with anything at all, then try to experience being with them as much as possible. It might be sitting in a pub with a bartender absolutely at one with her role or watching some world-class athletics live in a stadium. You might go to a play or a concert. The clues are only that there must be a high level of relevant skill, a lack of tension (alignment) and a lack of self-consciousness (attunement).*

What is stopping you?

Time to move on to our final room.

The Innermost Sanctum

Please spend time with *The Monk on the Mountain*

The Monk on the Mountain

John has spent a great deal of time in the mountains of China. The fact that he suffers from extreme vertigo to some might be seen as a problem, and they would be right. But good planning (and sitting on bus seats furthest away from the edge) seems to just about make getting to places doable. Mountain excursions for John are rare. His worst nightmare would be to have to climb a set of crumbling narrow steps that are cut into the sides of mountains. Sheer drops and slips that result in certain death are not his cup of tea.

An important mountain in the Wudang region is called Golden Top. As part of John's training, he has to experience the particular energy that can be found at its summit. In short – he really has to go. John is assured by the group that it is an easy six-hour ascent and that there are absolutely no mountain steps or sheer drops anywhere along the way. Evidently it's an internal climb. 'People go there all the time', he is told. This information comes from his colleagues who have been there before and so he feels safe to take the journey.

Five minutes before reaching the summit, John turns the corner to find himself on a ledge. He's not exactly sure how far he is from the edge, but he knows he must be close. John glances to the right where he sees steps carved into the side of the mountain. To make matters worse they are the only way to the top. It is not a long flight (which is why his friends forgot to mention them) but everything becomes too much for John to stomach and he vomits. It is not a case of whether he can climb the steps. It is a case of whether he can move from the spot he is in without collapsing. John finds himself entirely paralysed. His friends offer to stay with him or even to walk up the steps alongside him. But, as anyone with vertigo will tell you, watching someone else close to an edge produces exactly the same response as if you are standing there yourself – an overwhelming desire to die.

Eventually, John persuades his friends to go on without him. He knows that if he can just manage to stand by himself for half an hour he will almost certainly be able to develop the courage to turn around and head back to safety. It's a terrifying waiting game; one he has played only twice before (and obviously won). In both instances, he needed days to recover before being able to stand without shaking.

John is relieved that his friends have gone on without him. In this situation it is better that he is left entirely alone. Then something happens. An elderly monk, perhaps in his eighties, stops and looks at him. The monk asks John if he is okay. Out of extreme respect, John somehow manages to find the words to explain that he is afraid of heights – especially the stairs. Then the monk looks at John square in the eyes and gently says the following, meaning every word: 'Don't worry. I will carry you. I will carry you.'

There is a pause.

And, in that moment, John is so humbled by the offer, so touched by this aged man who has offered to carry him, so affected by the feel of the monk's strength of character, that he finds himself momentarily in a different space. He even attempts a smile but is not sure that it reaches his face. Then the monk puts out his arm as if to encourage him to go ahead, and somehow John is too grateful not to do it. He climbs the stairs despite his fear. It is as if something bigger and broader and more powerful than extreme fear itself has taken over. The offer is so authentically given that it moves John – and he is released.

John meets his friends on Golden Top, one of whom is kind enough to take a photograph that you might get to see some day. It is John sitting on a stone lotus. Directly behind him is a sheer drop of 3,000 feet. The effect is short lived, perhaps lasting for two hours or so, just enough time for John to experience Golden Top and to get down the tricky steps. Nevertheless, John's moment with the monk on the mountain remains to this day the gentlest, most matter of fact and effective coaching experience he has encountered. It represents a turning point, after which he was able to understand that a coach, a parent, a therapist, a leader or a teacher can inspire a healthier way of being beyond any benchmark he had previously known.

You may have guessed that John is me.

And, as I am here, allow me to escort you to the final room.

I wish you joy and luck in your practice.

I hope to meet with you in person sometime soon.

You arrive at the last door.

Room Nine

The most profound learning is found
in the ordinary – or what we have been
led to believe is ordinarily acceptable.

Will: Part One

Chang Li Wei's alarm buzzes at 4.50am. He pulls on his old T-shirt (always clean), his warm fleece hoody (not always clean as it takes too long to dry in the damp of the mountains), his Boss underwear (always clean) and his black cotton meditation pants bought from the mountain's tourist market. He's tired. The students who are more advanced than him always sleep peacefully every night. For them there is no dreaming whatsoever. But, for Chang Li Wei, especially at this altitude, and especially at his age of nineteen, dreams are a more vivid affair. This morning he wakes up exhausted, feeling like he's been on some kind of heroic adventure.

He grabs his pillow and blanket and heads out of his room. After a short walk, he comes to the meditation area to find the rest of his crowd. There are ten. The master is already sitting on the floor, cross-legged, supported on either side by cushions, two on one side and one on the other to protect his damaged knees. The pillows have been, as always, arranged by his assistant. He is Japanese, and next in line to receive the lineage. Chang Li Wei is grateful that his teacher is still around. Soon he will be disappearing into the wilderness of the mountains for three years for the final stage of his practice. There is only the craft of meditation for him. As usual, there is a white candle lit in the corner of the room and, behind it on the wall, a hand-painted scroll. A single incense stick fragrances the space with the slightest trace of jasmine.

Chang Li Wei remembers it's Saturday and a broad smile spreads across his face. 'Will,' he thinks, 'that lazy dumb head. Where the hell is he?' Chang Li Wei and Will are the youngest members of the bunch and are very close friends. They discuss everything together. Will is English and at school in China, which is why he can only join the group at weekends. He arrives very late on Friday night and usually stays until Sunday afternoon. This time it is the school holidays, so he will be boarding with Chang Li Wei for two whole weeks.

Right on cue, in shuffles Will, looking every inch the zombie that a sixteen-year-old skinny vegan boy tends to be at 5am. Hair floppy and curly at the same time. Both nod at each other, almost imperceptibly. You can tell instantly they are friends. Chang Li Wei smiles. Will sort of grunts. Chang Li Wei laughs. Will grunts again. The two young men sit down, comfortably close to each other, genuinely pleased to be where they are.

Chang Li Wei has a pillow supporting one knee and a rolled-up blanket propping up the other. His hips were injured as a young boy because an overzealous Kung Fu instructor pushed him too hard. He appreciates that the master regularly reminds the group that it is the quality of the meditation that counts and not the position they sit in. 'Greats such as the Dali Lama meditate sitting on a chair and are grateful for the support it offers.' Will, however, sits naturally and easily in full lotus. He and the floor are at one. The only other student in full lotus is the master's assistant who has been meditating since the age of four or five. She says that she has always loved sitting this way, much to the chagrin of her father who wanted her to sit at a desk and to focus on her studies.

The master takes three deep breaths and the class join in. Then Will and Chang Li Wei lean ever so slightly into their meditation positions as they have been taught to do. For the first part of this morning's session, the class are to hold their arms in specific positions for extended periods of time, while meditating. Imagine sitting on the floor and lifting your straight arms to the sides at shoulder height. Now imagine flexing your hands so your fingers are pointing to the ceiling. Now hold this position for an hour or two. Today, the master has demonstrated three positions that Chang Li Wei and Will must memorize because at some point during the meditation he will tell them to change their positioning from one to the next.

Chang Li Wei closes his eyes knowing that the technique requires him to forget entirely about his outstretched arms until he hears the instruction to move them. When he first began meditating, he was extremely excited by the type of imagery his mediations would produce. Often, he would seem to be taken on some kind of journey – through doors and the like. Then, one day, he plucked up the courage to tell the master about his wonderful experiences. The master looked at him with a pitiful expression and told him not to worry – sooner or later he'd stop being bothered by such interferences. That was a good lesson to learn.

It is meant to be impossible to go to sleep when one is meditating properly because the falling reflex kicks in and the shot of adrenaline it produces will always wake you up. However, nobody has told this to Will. Sometime into the session, in the still of the mountain morning, Chang Li Wei hears a gentle but familiar thud. He knows that next to him is a sixteen-year-old teenager, sitting in the lotus position, bent impossibly forwards with the top of his head resting on the floor. Soon there will be the sound of gentle snoring. Chang Li Wei doesn't need to open his eyes to know that everyone, including the master, is smiling and lifted because of Will, and that their morning meditations are enriched because of him.

Will: Part Two

Twice a year, the group are visited by adventure holiday makers. Today is one of those days and the tourists arrive at the building disgruntled. Their hotel is an entire kilometre from the building and they have had to walk. Chang Li Wei enjoys new people joining the group. It brings a different type of energy. This time the party are a particularly strange bunch. Amongst them are a martial arts student and his master. The student has come to the mountains to stay for a while to improve his form, and the master has tagged along. A concept alien to Chang Li Wei. Shouldn't it be the other way around? Someone else, Derek, amuses Chang Li Wei. Derek is convinced he is being told what to do by his solar plexus. It speaks to him in words. Derek tells Chang Li Wei that his solar plexus has never once let him down, but the tour leader tells him that Derek has got lost so many times on the trip, wandering off while following his solar plexus' instructions, that she has concerns for his safety. There is Gladys from the USA whose sole interest is the photography of orbs. She says to Chang Li Wei that they are spirits in the form of spheres of light, invisible to the naked eye. She has a special camera to snap them. There is also Pete who never goes anywhere without his flask of tea. He doesn't ever want to be thirsty. 'Thirst is a sign that the body is lacking water, you know.' There is also another lady, Barbara, who is missing her pet hamster and thinking of returning home early.

When the time comes for meditation practice, the tour group walk quickly into the room, rushing ahead of the regular students to get to the front. Only Derek sits by the door at the back, just in case his solar plexus tells him to leave. The ones at the front, in their pristine meditation gear, sit in their awkward lotus positions ready to begin. The master kindly explains to them that the lotus isn't necessary, but none move an inch because they feel they know better. They've read many books on the subject and watched YouTube videos. The regular students find a place somewhere in the middle and towards the back.

When everybody is ready, the master initiates the session by giving his instruction. Most of the new group put on a demonstration of exaggerated listening. There's lots of wise nodding accompanied by loud deep breathing in preparation for the enormity of what they are about to do. This particular type of breathing is something new to Chang Li Wei. Evidently it is called 'centring'. The regular students simply listen as normal people do, knowing that their breath will naturally slow during the meditation. And when it does, they will move to reverse breathing to deepen the meditative experience. The tour group, now thinking they know better than the master, have already stopped listening and are rearranging the paraphernalia around them. Chang Li Wei wonders how they are going to know what to do. The answer is they don't, and the master must explain again answering many unnecessary questions.

As the meditation begins, there is quite a lot of coughing from the new group. Evidently this is a 'thing'. Fifteen minutes in, as things start to become a little challenging, Derek's solar plexus conveniently tells him to leave, and so he does, shutting the door loudly behind him. Half an hour later, there is the sound of someone opening a flask. Pete has become thirsty and has stopped meditating for a cup of tea. At this point the newcomers are already struggling to hold their lotus positions and are beginning to tut and sigh as if their problems are somebody else's fault. Some even stand up to clear the cramp in their legs. After just an hour of sitting the master decides it's time to bring the meditation to a halt.

Coming out of meditation can be a delicate time. In the case of deep meditation, it can be very dangerous and students have been known to become lost. With this in mind the master, as usual, speaks slowly and firmly as he guides the energy back towards the body and then into the place where it can be safely stored. All of a sudden, up jumps Gladys who runs around the room flashing her camera in a frantic attempt to capture her invisible orbs that she senses must be there.

While the other interruptions are harmless, Gladys' is not, and afterwards the master has a quiet word with her together with the tour group leader to explain the gravity of the situation and the possible dangers of her actions to the other more experienced students. 'I have paid for this vacation and I'm at a stage in my life when I can do what I damn well want,' replies Gladys before storming off, partly angered at being told what to do, and partly angered that her digital camera shows not a glimmer of an orb. After the master has left the regulars stand around. Chang Li Wei and Will take some photos into the air of the dim room with their phones. The photos are full of orbs. You cannot see anything else but orbs. They find Gladys and show her the images. She rushes back to the room but yet again leaves empty-handed.

Will: Part Three

The next morning, Will is nowhere to be seen. He misses early meditation and when he misses breakfast too (something Will never does) Chang Li Wei goes to check up on his friend. The bed is empty. 'Ah,' thinks Chang Li Wei, remembering it is the school holidays, 'he must have taken himself off on an adventure.' Will sometimes does this when the mood is right, walking where the wind takes him, buying food where he can, or begging where he can't. It's not unusual. He is such a charming lad. He never goes hungry. 'Will always leaves his phone behind,' remembers Chang Li Wei, 'ah. There it is, on his bed.' Chang Li Wei proceeds to give Will's parents a call to let them know the situation. They, of course, have no concerns for their lad. He is sensible and knows to stick to the path.

A day or so later, the visitors start to notice that Will isn't there. They find out from Chang Li Wei that he has gone off for a while on his own into the mountains. They run to the master and demand to know where Will is. How could the master be so irresponsible as to let him go? He's only sixteen. The master replies simply with a shrug. Taking this as a sign of heartless non-caring, the group begin to question their own safety on the mountain and they grow more and more outraged. They can't believe it. It wouldn't happen in their country. Chang Li Wei goes to them and explains that Will has done this sort of thing before and is very likely to be okay. They do not like the phrases 'done this sort of thing before' and 'very likely' at all, and mutter amongst themselves fervently. Chang Li Wei tells them that Will's parents know of the situation and are happy for their son to go. For some reason the muttering increases.

As the day wears on, the idea of becoming holiday heroes starts to permeate the group. They dismiss common sense because it interferes with the stories they are now dying to tell about how they saved the boy. By the evening, the group's momentum is going at full speed, albeit down a rabbit hole, crushing anything logical in its path. 'The poor boy must be lost. Lost. And it is dark! How will he find his way home?' At 11pm, in the pitch black of the night, on a mountain they know nothing of, they launch a search party for Will. Chang Li Wei tries to explain to them the dangers of the dark, but the group tell him they are the only ones who really care for the boy and 'something must be done. It must. He's lost. Lost!'

First out is Derek with his solar plexus guiding the way. Straight into a boulder and nearly off the edge of the mountain he goes. Thankfully, even while posturing as heroes, the group do think to go in pairs and Pete is there to stop him falling down. Some think Will may have slipped into a crevasse and, with no climbing equipment, attempt a dangerous descent to see if he is there.

After two hours, the energy and commitment needed for the search takes its toll and the group's efforts dwindle. Their mission becomes a slow walk occasionally calling into the quiet of the mountain night, 'Will. Wiiiillll.' The group return to base, two by two. 'At least we tried,' they said, and gave each other a round of applause. Exhausted, they decide that sleep is the best option for now and they arrange to regroup the next day. Most go to bed tired but happy. They are on the adventure holiday they have secretly craved – saving a lost boy, hopefully with minimal effort.

The next morning, after waking up late around noon, they meet to decide what to do next. It does not seem to occur to them that the peace and light of the morning might be the most productive time for a search. Derek's solar plexus is playing up and has told him to stay in bed for the rest of the day. He does so tucked up with his boxes of biscuits that are not for sharing. After much discussion the group eventually decide to get some posters printed offering a reward for the safe return of Will. After all, he may, of course, have been kidnapped. Chang Li Wei tells them that the reward they are offering is worth five years' salary to most of the shop owners on the mountain and perhaps they should lower it. This advice they choose to ignore.

Later that day, after the first few posters have been placed with excited shop owners who close up to join the search, news comes that Will has been found. He is staying at a monastery some fifteen kilometres away. One of the shop keepers who regularly delivers to that place on the mountain has spotted him meditating in the grounds and is now going to fetch him back on his bike. True to his word, a few hours later, up cycles a smiling shop owner and, on the back, a rather bewildered Will. The group are beside themselves with joy at their achievement. They have found the lost boy and have brought him back safe and sound. Their jubilant celebrations shatter the peace of the mountain.

Will: Part Four

Then things start to darken. The group turn on Will, and their true natures emerge. They are not aligned with spiritual goodness but instead with the force of the black and grey that fills the space behind the façade. Barely has Will had a chance to get off the bike and to thank the owner when the group seem to form some type of orderly queue in front of him. Each is deeply angry about what Will has 'put us through'. 'We risked our lives for you,' they say in their own ways. Their alignment with their darkness attacks from behind with direct and immediate force. It has a life of its own, crushing any façade in its path. It is the sharpest knife stabbing and the fastest bullet piercing.

The group are systematic in their approach. They take it in turns to go at the boy. Chang Li Wei does not recognise the truth in the words they keep repeating: 'I just want to tell you how I feel'. What he sees instead is their false front crumbling, something the truly vicious hide behind. Some shout bitterly and resentfully, sending arrows into Will, only to give him a hug afterwards and to say that they do not bear grudges. 'All is forgotten now.' Others are more subtle and are merely 'disappointed' in him, but their darkness cuts past any barriers that Will can summon and penetrates the lad deeply.

To Chang Li Wei, it is as if these people contain a malicious spirit that periodically emerges when their spiritual front collapses. It is as if the contrivance of pretending to be spiritual, of convincing themselves and others that they are at one with something they are not, takes so much energy that it is similar to a mountain with a bubbling volcano waiting underneath. When it finally cracks and explodes, it does so with one of the most destructive forces in nature. It is the demon that exists in the 'false heart', bursting out of its cage. It is the pain of the pretence of love, of the pretence of joy, of the absence of the 'true heart'. And it is with this force that the group knock the lad down until he is barely breathing. They feel it is their privilege and their duty to do so.

The next day, after a lunch of weak soup and rice, the group leave for home. 'The mountain hasn't touched them at all,' thinks Chang Li Wei, as he waves goodbye and heads to his favourite spot to sit for a while. When he returns, he finds Will sitting outside with a cup of tea. Chang Li Wei smiles and sits too, delighted to see his friend, but Will is not his usual self. Chang Li Wei pats Will's hand as if to say it's okay. As it turns out, it is not okay. It is not okay at all.

Will does not come to the afternoon or evening meditations, even though these are the times he loves. Instead, he chooses to sleep. The next morning, Will enters the room stony-faced and serious. He is energetically altered – damaged. The room feels different to Chang Li Wei, and so it is. After the meditation, Will politely bows to the master and leaves. An hour later, he picks up his bags, cadges a lift down the mountain, and heads home. The lad will eventually return, and his recovery will happen over time, mostly because of his friend. But, for the time being, Will is gone and the group are poorer for it.

Chang Li Wei has witnessed an attempt on the destruction of youth by adults; an attempt on the destruction of innocence by those who seek to educate; an attempt on the destruction of the vulnerable by those in power, of those with ego pretending to lead the virtuous way. Chang Li Wei suddenly has visions of all the teachers who are putting on a front; he sees all of the coaches and counsellors whose focus on the explainable inhibits those with so much hope and ambition to be great or to be cured;

he wonders whether things being unintentional are a valid excuse for harm. But, most of all, Chang Li Wei wonders at the nature of the darkness – at how those unaligned with the light seem naturally and consistently driven to pull others down into their private abyss.

And then Chang Li Wei sees his master, who does nothing but uplift without a word, who would never say, 'It's time you grew up', who builds and never destroys and who is the toughest task master he knows…

...and then Chang Li Wei turns to you and says,
'You can be part of the silent, invisible, unstoppable,
unrestricted movement of change.' And he adds,
'You no longer need to say there isn't a way.'

All you need to do is to be less acquired today
than you were the day before.

You are the creator of the environment.

When you are ready.

Open the door to the light of day.

Step outside.

Take a breath.

You know that this is not the end.

About the Author

Dr John Rowe, DProf, B.Ed, ALAM hons, is a doctor of coaching, a leadership master coach, a specialist counsellor and a mentor. In his twenties, he danced at the Moulin Rouge in Paris. In his thirties and forties, he taught and led in a wide variety of schools. Now, John is one of the most established coaches of senior leaders in schools in the UK. Much travelled, John currently enjoys spending a bit more time at home in his small cottage on a Leicestershire farm, meditating, writing and generally gallivanting around.